Kent Johnson is an avant-garde poet without an avant-garde.

– Keith Tuma, *Chicago Review*

[Johnson] continues an avant-garde project that values 'a revolt against art, morality, and society.' Such a 'revolt' for Johnson is centered predominantly on how collective ideologies and national narratives shape artistic, moral, and social values. By bringing new perspectives in his satire into collision with received poetic practices, Johnson challenges contemporary poets to consider more carefully their commitments to audiences in diverse public situations. He asks also that they adapt their words and images to the particular requirements of social and political situations. The public and private spaces wherein larger national narratives and ideologies are processed by observers of foreign and domestic policy become significant staging grounds wherein poetry can be used to influence belief and desire.

– Dale Smith, *Jacket*

Kent Johnson....is my favorite American author.

– Semezdin Mehmedinović

Kent Johnson takes a scalpel to the formation of our ideological consciousness in a poetry that matters more and more as it maps, investigates, and interrogates just how we got where we are.

– Ammiel Alcalay

Lyrical, taut, amused, seeing, pissed. Kent Johnson's poems make me uncomfortable. And uncomfortable in a good way.

– Hoa Nguyen

The provocation of Johnson's poetic is not an end in itself. Instead, he repeatedly challenges our most basic assumptions about what poetry can (and cannot) do.

– Bill Freind, *Denver Quarterly*

Johnson represents our fiendish blind spots, the nature of those far cries of human murderousness alongside the fragility of identity and dignity…in hope of replenishing the means of our deliverance.

– Lissa Wolsak

Kent Johnson's texts are like unchained pit bulls tossed into a school yard—somebody is going to get bit… Over the years since I first met him in Leningrad, I have been both impressed & appalled at his hijinks, often both at once.

– Ron Silliman

You must walk with this book, open it and read it in all your different moods: it will reflect all of them. It is both heartwarming and heart breaking. There is a simultaneous joy and melancholy to Johnson's writing, which, of course, even as it is prose, we expect from the most urgent poems of our times.

– Benjamin Hollander, *Entropy*

With Kent Johnson's new book against my breast I am pulled to the broken window and the night mist and bus exhaust and the next thirty years that will happen to all of us.

– Farid Matuk

Homage to the Pseudo Avant-Garde

Homage
to the
Pseudo Avant-Garde

One Hundred and Sixty-Five Poems
(2008-2016)

Kent Johnson

Spuyten Duyvil
Dispatches Editions

Most of these poems appeared, some in slightly different versions, in the following locales: *Both Both, Chicago Review, Claudius App, Denver Quarterly, Dispatches from the Poetry Wars, Harpur's Palate, Isola di Rifiuti, Journal of Poetic Research, Letras en línea* (Chile), *Mandorla, Sous les Pavés.*

A good number of them have been included in chapbooks or books published by the following presses: Beard of Bees, BlazeVox Books, Effing Press, Habenicht Press, Delete Press, Longhouse Books, Starcherone Books.

My warmest thanks to all the initial publishers of writings included in this present collection.

Copyright, © Kent Johnson, 2017.

ISBN 978-1-944682-33-0

Library of Congress Cataloging-in-Publication Data applied for.

Dispatches Editions is an imprint of Spuyten Duyvil Press.

Titles in this series available at online distributors and via

dispatchespoetry.com

spuytenduyvil.net

*Dedicación a Benjamin Hollander,
siempre presente en nuestra poesía*

Contents

Preface 11
Recent and Unbound Poems 13
Homage to Villon 47
From *Works and Days of the fénéon collective* 61
The Rejection Group Texts 69
The Ashbery Mystery 89
From *I Once Met*, 2nd Edition 99
Doggerel for the Masses 139
Prize List [Second Version] 165

Coda: Vanguard Socialist Realism 171

Preface

Satire has been around almost as long as stupidity, and it's safe to say that stupidity has been around as long as humans, which makes both part of our defining condition. Mind you, there is probably considerably more stupidity around now than there was in the Pleistocene, if only because back then it no doubt got you eliminated from the gene pool pretty quickly. *Har har, did you see that idiot walk into the tar pit without looking?* Now it gets you promoted to some position where you can effectively screw things up and blame it on the people under you. Or run for President of the U.S.A. while claiming the whole thing is rigged. Or build a professional poetry Empire while claiming to be the avant-garde. While stupidity (and its constant companion, hypocrisy) surrounds us, it's difficult to put your finger on exactly what it is. Even Avitol Ronell who wrote the book on it, admits as much. "While stupidity is 'what is there,'" she writes, "it cannot be simply located or easily scored."

It can, however, be skinned, skewered, roasted, and hung out to dry. That's where Kent Johnson comes in. If we can't define stupidity, we can certainly expose it, and in exposing it, weaken it, even if we can never do away with it. That is the moral drive of satirists like Johnson, which rarely makes them instantly popular. From Ben Franklin's wicked critique of the hypocrisy of preaching liberty while enslaving yourself to debt in order to buy stuff you can't afford and don't need; to Mark Twain's take-no-prisoners savaging of Christian slave owners; to H.L. Mencken, Lenny Bruce, Richard Prior, Jon Stewart, Sarah Silverstein, and Negin Farsad, satire has been a source of resistance to the brutality and viciousness of U.S. national policies at home and abroad. Less often, it has also targeted the continuing hypocrisy and collaboration of various social and artistic formations who fiddle away looking for government money, ignoring the patriarchy that sells "liberty" and "democracy" overseas as part of an expansionist legerdemain, even as that same culturally beneficent government guns down unarmed black men in its own streets.

English language poetry, though, for more than a couple hundred years, has had a hard time keeping up with satire. The satirical poetry of Pope and Dryden sank beneath the wave of Romanticism's egotistical sublime and never really recovered as an honoured form. Edward Dorn was an exception. A student of the 18th century, Dorn drew a bead on the stupidities of the mid-20th century U.S. with an acute intelligence and an unshakable moral centre. Mostly, however, the post-New American Poetry landscape devolved into a world divided between the post-post-Romantic, Amy Lowell-esque lyrics of the ubiquitous MFA and Creative Writing programs and the formalist postures of a self-commodified avant-garde jockeying for university positions and government money (any government, including the most repressive like late-Stalinist China).

Following Dorn's lead, Kent Johnson is a marked exception to that bleak situation. Since he began publishing in the 1980's, he has produced a stream of satirical work that equals Dorn's (and certainly gets a nod of approval from Mark Twain) in its relentless revelation of the hypocrisy thriving in contemporary life. In books like *Lyric Poetry after Auschwitz*, *Doggerel for the Masses*, and *Homage to the Last Avant-Garde*, Johnson has laid bare the cruel stupidities that have enabled vicious wars and domestic injustice and violence, confronting them with fearless honesty and moral clarity and a good deal of side splitting humour. The title poem of one of those books, "Lyric Poetry after Auschwitz," is among the most powerful anti-war poems written in the last century. In addition, Johnson is intimately associated with a number of unprecedented Events which he has produced and/or participated in which have disturbed the self-satisfied equanimity of the Literary Establishment (not least the Professional Avant-Garde), laying bare their empty aesthetic rhetoric, ridiculous posturing, and shameless careerism, at a time when more than ever we need clarity of vision.

Homage to the Pseudo Avant-Garde offers that clarity, bringing together much of Johnson's work since 2008 with more recent compositions, including some that engage the 2016 U.S. Election Farce/Tragedy. The sheer diversity of the writing is a joy. It is first-power poetry, even when it doesn't look like poetry, and that is central to its ongoing pleasure. Johnson's energy and enthusiasm constantly give rise to new forms, including bumper sticker verse, micro essays and biographies, procedural compositions, strict iambic meters, essays, and straight ahead lyric. He is always political without trying to be. The moral/political vision is steeped in his bones so that every word resonates with it without effort. Johnson radically breaches the patrolled boundaries of genre over and over even as he articulates an uncompromisingly honest revelation of the stupidities that surround us and inform us. In our current era with its Reality Television ontology and its universal commodification and professionalization of poetry, Johnson offers a fresh take on the world. Read on and thrill to the brilliance of this *oner* from Illinois.

Michael Boughn
24 October 2016

Recent and Unbound Poems

Let Us Now Give Thanks to the New American Poetry

Something happened to me at the waterpark.
– Allen Tate

Prelude

Not that anyone would or should
care for my fickle poetic leanings,
but I've elected now to share, half
naked and pickled as I'm presently
feeling (I'll explain), some thoughts
about some things, that these thoughts
might flutter about, with errant and
rowdy wings, while the mind is juiced.
So to begin and without further fanfáre,
I'll just say so: that Mayakovsky and
Vallejo, fair poets of the hammer and
the sickle, are pillars in my heart,
without compare. And yet on other days,
alas, and at prevalent spells for near a
week, or two, I will seek a book by the
crook Villon, or the classical Greek
Cavafy; Yea, my poetical desiring is
queer and fleeting. Randomly, I think
of a variety: the grumpy sorceress
Moore, or the gorgeously enflamed
Césaire, or the sassy commie Dalton,

or the wacky virtuoso Di Giorgio, say,
from Uruguay, where I spent my youth
and later went back, as fate would play,
to work as a gym instructor at the
YMCA. Which makes me think, I don't
know why; I've wondered it before, and
my wondering again is envisioned:
Shouldn't certain U.S. poets stop mooching
on State-sponsored tours in Stalinist China,
where numerous poets are imprisoned?
And now a meditation concerning Japan, if
I may: Is it uncouth (which rhymes above
with youth) for an ex-Trot WASP, like me,
to propound that the minimalist stuff of an
itinerant, alcoholic, apolitical, Meiji-Taishō
Zen haikuist is way more profound and
universal than any prototypical Academic-
Po-Cult-Capital-Speculation fluff?

1.
No doubt it is (uncouth), but hold on,
Mongrel Coalition, why is my heart
skipping beats, is this ventricular fibrillation?
Alright, now it's stopped. Hot men
and women of all colors go back to
baring hot bodies at the waterpark
with their breasts and bikini bottoms.

Is that bad to say, Stasi Po-police of
today? Au contraire, I declare. I mean,
look at that taut ass – is Desire not a radical
Good? Around her/him all that is solid
melts into air. But to return to my subject,
from this metal and rubber reclining chair:
I've been reading Taneda Santōka's bone-
marrow-haiku by this pool, in Wisconsin
Dells. I'm to give an out-loud reading
tomorrow, at a water park resort, believe
it or not (another one down the road—there
are quite a few of them here, right off I-90).
It's sponsored by the Wisconsin Dells
Acker Poetry Belles, you will scarcely
believe it. I'm really quite enjoying being
here, among the Packer crowd, before the
shtick, sipping an Old Fashioned, the third
or fourth, I admit, though some kids with
green and gold life-preserver bubbles on
their stick-like limbs are screaming very
loud before their childhood dies and rots
away, like Emma Bovary's, and the world,
as well; it's like the empty, translucent
shells of Ashbery's cicadas: They can't do
anything about it, nor can you. Why does
the blue jet of liquid jet into the blue?

2.
Anyway, Santōka was writing in the
late Twenties and, yes, he was in his
late twenties, then, too; the haiku
Field was riven by infidel revolt:
It was Haiku-Dada-Time, one could
say. All the vanguard Japanese poets
were young and it was like there was a
mad dash to immolate their youths on
command from some vengeful blue-
liquid-jet God in the *Man'yōshū,* and
then whoosh, youth's season was gone
in a flash. That's how life is, kids, no
rhyme or reason, deep down beneath sad
biology. So would you please just keep it
down, I'm trying to write something about

3.
ideology. OK, forget it. At any rate,
there were, like, huge, blinding flashes
in the sky that had never been
experienced before by human
beings. And then the New American
Poetry appeared all of a sudden,
or so it seemed, to the people in
their twenties standing there,
amazed, within it. They too were

very young and full of life, as life
was full of them. Not that things didn't
happen in the Thirties and Forties:
There was Gertrude Stein writing
speeches for Pétain; the Fugitives
took their stand for slavery; Pound
was screaming darkly in Italy; dark

4.
antennae began to get densely
planted on round summits; tons of
kids got washed out of turrets with
hoses at waterparks in Pushkin's
Russia and Rilke's Prussia, and so
forth and so on. But the New Americans
were the loaded gunners and a half in
follow-up, for sure: They went
bonkers against poetry getting mixed
up with Academic Institutions and
State and corporate money and
slavish position-jockeying and
stuff, as it was, back then, in
proto, with the New Critics. They

5.
were stick-in-the-muds, the
New Americans, I guess you
could put it, quasi-Ultra types,
party poopers, some might opine,
not hip at all on cash bars at
MLA-time and like-Academic
decorum. Say what you want about
their anarchist-line and righteous
zealotry, but had it not been for
them, Post-Avant American poetry
would be in ten pickles of trouble
presently, let me tell you, far
from the wild and sovereign and
honorable spirit that guides the
Field today, thank God, against
the careerist and protocoled
rituals we've all so wisely

6.
eschewed. Because, thankfully,
the New Americans showed us
how it's done—how to fashion
scruffy Autonomous Poetic
Zones against the grain of
career-clubby dispensations; how
to defy capitulation; how to

resist the siren suctions of
the Culture Industry, as Emily
Dickinson more or less urged,
in a poem about slave auctions;
how to refuse being a pawn in the
Rules of the Game; how to forbear
being a species of courtier. Phew!
True, granted, the French/Belgian
Surrealists and the Mexico City
Infrarrealists and the Black Arts

7.
axis helped us to refine our praxis
(so what, we're internationalists,
we don't care who came up with
the key ideas, we don't have to
pretend we own it all). And not that
it's all sunny skies at the waterpark,
to coin a phrase, because, sure,
there are two or three sell-outs, still,
hanging around, pretending they're
insurrectionists; you'll always have
a few lame apples in the bushel; that
kind of outlier aberration is assumed:
It's one of those Rules of the Game,
as we know post-Husserl.

8.
So all in all, we're in luck: For were it
not for the New American Poetry, we
Post-Avant American poets would, if
you think about it, possibly be the
laughingstock of Literary History two
hundred years from now(!), like those
Georgians or Firesides or New Critics we
mock today, with their enormous beards
and muttonchops so big you could muck
around in there for a week, like Hansel
and Gretel at the AWP, just to get eaten
by the Witch of Fuck. Sorry, I mean those
ancient guys who thought they were so

9.
avant-garde and all that, when
really they were totally funky
bunkum? Can you imagine *our*
ending up that way, as a group
or period, our architecture all
antique looking, with slender or
thick postmodern columns, and
wall surfaces with pilasters and
decorative features, including
sculpted déjà vu figurines in
frozen, Mannerist pirouettes at

the top of the edifice? Well,
thankfully, we've learned key
lessons from the New American
poetry! These kids won't shut up,
dammit, but kids will be kids, it's
not like their screaming means
they'll be timid bourgeois sell-outs
when they get old, they're just
kids. But I wish the green and gold
bubble-devices around their arms
would pop all at once, that would be
fun, and give some drama to this ersatz

10.
Wave Pool. No, just kidding. I
don't really want any kids to
drown. They are so blithely
content, rising and falling, there,
innocent as the soon-dead day,
which now spreads overhead,
magnificent, its orange and mauve
gown. It's like there's been a
traumatic shipwreck but everyone
is ecstatic. Keep looking up, I say,
and don't look down. So, OK, that's
enough from me: Let us now give thanks
to the New American poetry.

Forgotten American Poets of the 19th Century

– for John Bradley, in the 21st

Absalom William Moore is a poet who thought poetry was an anchor in the drift of the world.

Adelaide Mary Brown is a poet who inspired strong feelings among the bachelors of her town.

Bartholomew Derrick Taylor is a poet who spoke to us intimately, from an almost suffocating nearness.

Obedience Sophie Walker is a poet who believed there's another world where we will read to each other high on a mountain in the wind.

Cuthbert Eli Morgan is a poet who always seemed to connect with the choir.

Abiah Charlotte Sanders is a poet who spun her gold down through the moving deep laurel shade all day.

Chauncey Thaddeus Powell is a poet who believed that there are no grounds for belief.

Lucretia Florence Jenkins is a poet who believed they will have to believe it as we believed it.

Cornelius August Parker is a poet who thought he was lit up like morning glories and was showered by the rain of his symbols.

Cyrus Wiley Butler is a poet who believed long poems are "much closer to a whole reality" than shorter poems, but too late.

Fredonia Anna Ross is a poet who believed she had spent the afternoon blowing soap bubbles.

Obediah Virgil Foster is a poet who believed the day was gloves.

Hester Wilma Campbell is a poet who was suddenly covered at the party by the wasps of the doorsill.

Ebenezer Charles Freeman is a poet whose last words were "The pool is covered in slime."

Permelia Margaret Holmes is a poet who believed that when a screen door banged in the wind it made one of her hinges come loose.

Epaphroditus Benjamin Warren is a poet who didn't and doesn't really care where poetry is now.

Prudence Alice Grant is a poet who rode a mule until the mule had to be carried.

Phineas Derrick Knight is a poet who thought of himself highly, believing the nature of what is personal imitates oblivion.

Temperance Clarissa Hamilton is a poet who wrote poems in French with the design that they be translated into the English of the Queen.

Hiram Josiah Hunt is a poet who dragged a rotten log from the bottom of a stagnant pond.

Jedediah Louis Mason is a poet who nested at the end of a tunnel, where he was discovered beneath a bank.

Elijah Aquilla Burns is a poet who loved Rochester, and who flows northward like two joined sewers.

Zachariah Thomas Hayes is a poet who believed we go back to poems as to a wife, leaving the boyfriend we desire.

Malvina Penelope Smith is a poet who shouted primitive slogans and shot symbolic smoke out her gills.

Olive Martha Weaver is a poet who believed she could simply choose to "wander away" from an optional apocalypse.

Nathaniel Edward East is a poet who wondered how the singing of the housefinch rings in finchskull, which wondering made him mad.

Electa Joan McCoy is a poet who believed it was a misunderstanding, mud sliding from the side where the thing was let in.

Mabel Ellen Greene is a poet who believed the whole brilliant mass comes spattering down.

Hezekiah Zander Fox is a poet whose two stalks pushed from the brain, through a series of miraculous infoldings to form optic cups.

Kesiah Relief Riley is a poet whose hair was black, and whose eyes were black, and from whose long fingers the spirits were conjured.

Newton Duncan Stone is a poet who believed Orpheus liked the glad personal quality of the things beneath the sky, which on that strange day began to rain frogs.

Isaac Davis Gibson is a poet who had a cow's head on his shoulders and candles sprouting from his back.

Abigail Isabel Hicks is a poet who has disappeared into libraries, into microfilm.

Jeremiah Cross Shaw is a poet who went mad and had relations with Longfellow, his steed.

Tryphosia Sybrina Chapman is a poet who believed our jousting ends in music, like saplings do, after a typhoon.

Loretta Judith Porter is a poet who liked it when it was snowing in Paris, a city which does not exist.

Priscilla Elinamifia Woods is a poet who wrapped you in the burnoose of memories against the dark temptations of the flesh.

Francis Quiet Bryant is a poet who entered the forest, followed a path, and was eaten by The Bear, or The Witch.

Judah Robert Daniels is a poet who discovered a way to translate Eastern texts so that Western men could read Orientally, down at the beach of agates.

Lafayette Blessed Strongly is a poet who thought he was ahead of his time, but now he is regarded as apocryphal.

Pleasant Reunion Washington is a poet whose last line was "I don't think the leeches are sucking anymore."

Jackson Auction Black is a poet whose classical meters were all blasted to ruins in defense of Charleston.

Henrietta Troy Mills is a poet who was stolen by the Apache and became an Apache, it is rumored.

Edward Azariah Cole is a poet who knew he would show them, those who had laughed and mocked him, but alas.

Anne Liza Bishop is a poet who insisted on signing Anonymous and so forever does.

Martha Damaris Tucker is a poet who did not doubt that her hands or her whole body were hers, as the grain of sand to the haboob or the shrimp to the tsunami.

Winifred Fullest Hart is a poet who, like Thomas Jefferson, saw grass enough for myriads of oxen to grind between their teeth.

Kenward Linwood Johnson is a poet who at one end of his line had a knot, and at the other end a hook, and he sat fishing for a camel until he was called to come back.

Experience April Weaver is a poet whose sorrow was so wide you couldn't see across it, if sorrow could be seen.

Forgotten American Poets of the 20th Century
[aborted eclogue]

> *"Sometimes I wonder what will happen to me."*
> –Janna Levin, particle astrophysicist

Piers

I ask that poet 33 be put back on the table, he did as he was able. The river bed is sandy and the water races along; the material synthesized in the centers of stars gets ejected back out into space when the star dies. Everyone tries. I ask that poeta triginta tres be put back on the table.

Cuddie

I ask that poet 15 be put back on the table, the horses have fled the stable. The front of the hut slides open, and the woman just sits there, staring out; dominant structures pull on their subordinate neighbors, causing small local motions against the background expansion. He died over his scansion. I ask that poeta quindecim be put back on the table.

Piers

I move that poet 501 be put back in circulation, there's no need for oblivion. Eventually, the prayer halls and all the icons they contain are pulled down; the hole is marked by a singularity: in other words spacetime is infinitely curved down a nozzle in the core. She couldn't have suffered more. I move that poeta quingenti unus be put back in circulation.

Cuddie

I beg that poet 247 be entered into conversation, he wrote with deep conviction. As I said, the pilots are pretty inexperienced, and nine times out of ten they crash their planes upside down; fifteen billion years later, we're here. He couldn't make it cohere. I beg that poeta ducenti quadraginta septem be entered into conversation.

Piers

I demand that poet 99 be rescued from nothingness, save her memory from emptiness. Boiling is done in enormous cauldrons that belong to the boss; from this perspective, as observers and performers of thought experiments, we can chart out the field on which we live. She wrote out her heart and had nothing left to give. I demand that poeta nonaginta novem be rescued from nothingness.

Cuddie

I plead that poet 12.3 be redeemed by the young critics, his oblivion is described by no existing physics. True, where the main car park in the center of town is today there used to be row upon row of eel baskets, strung right across the water; this space has handles which we could not see any more than the inhabitants of a torus could see the handle of their manifold surround. Like a tree with no one around, he fell without a sound. I plead that poeta duodecim punctum tres be redeemed by the young critics.

Piers

I implore that poet 57 be returned to the Norton, she is now so forgotten. Incidentally, it's the custom at funerals in our village for the family to scatter coins about in front of their house and in the temple; we are the product of this universe, and I think it can be argued that the entire cosmic code is imprinted in our brains. She laid down on the track and was run over, repeatedly, by trains. I implore that poeta quinquaginta septem be returned to the Norton.

Cuddie

I urge that poet 756 be returned to the podium, he won a MacArthur and appeared on Nickolodeon. In those days, people slept with their heads on wooden box pillows—the test was to sneak into a room where someone was sleeping and saw the pillow in half lengthwise very carefully; I suppose the life of the academic topologist is so good sometimes it seems ridiculous to complain. He died in a shack on the coast of Maine. I urge that poeta septingentos quinquaginta sex be returned to the podium.

Piers

I petition that poet 11,942 be salvaged from the vacuum, her concepts and marketing have dissolved into talcum. Poetry is mountainous and its forests are hard to reach, but in these times there is plenty of brush on flat land for people to harvest; the hot and cold spots are etched into the background radiation as light climbs out of the hills and hollows. Around her Goth optics, grad students flitted like swallows. I petition that poeta undecim milia nongenti quadraginta et duo be salvaged from the vacuum.

Cuddie

I entreat that poet 72,519 be raised from time's cellar, his doggerel, once so hipster, was a stunning bestseller. Ironically, I'd thought to tie a large piece of cloth around the boy's waist just in case he was dragged away by the tide; the infinite curvature that relativity predicts raises to the surface all kinds of weird quantum phenomena. He streaked across the sky to die at a community college in Oklahoma. I entreat that poeta septuaginta duo milia centum decem et novem be raised from time's cellar.

Piers

I insist that poet 146.8 be forgiven for his treason, his avant-garde red weather is now the Official season. In summer, the poets wear white uniforms and carry short swords with gleaming scabbards, while in winter they wear dark blue tunics, with short capes over their shoulders; if one tosses magnetic shavings in the presence of a magnetic field, the shavings will gather along the field lines, showing the presence, direction, and shape of said unseen field. The name of an actual war ciriminal was imprinted on his shield. I insist that poet centum quadraginta sex punctum octo be forgiven for his treason.

Piers and Cuddie as One

Now we are very tired and you, of course, are tired, too. And so we determine to bid you adieu. For so many, alas, forgotten have been, and so many more as well shall be, that such strange eclogue as ours, forsooth, could never, ever cease. Another thing is that today you have breeders producing chickens on a massive scale, not like it used to be, when farmers only kept a few birds; the bright star burns out, becoming a black vortex that fades invisibly against the darkness of space. O, poets, our art does make of us one eternal race. And so we part with these rhymes of bittersweet scent, may they lend some gentle grace to our great predicament:

Forget thee, poet, never! 'till the sun shall in glory cease to shine, and this earthly sphere shall melt beneath the wrath divine; when the stars that twinkle bright shall long have ceased to be the light of lonely mariners, over love's tempestuous sea; when all that is bright and beautiful has fled each sacred spot, Oh, then—and not 'till then—shalt thou ever, by Poetry, be forgot!

Let's Go Out and Tear Up the Town

Frank and Kenneth and Jimmy were driving
Back from a long trip to all of the rivers of the world.
A person had said to them, by the Nile, How old
Are you? And they had said As old as you. And she
Had said Oh, that's a great age, I remember it now,
As she moved past and away on a long, thin boat. But
Now the Sun was shimmering through the smog.
The nouns were struck, moved, changed. They sighed
When the car went through them with a sigh. The city
Sure seems different said Frank, We've been gone
For so long. Yes said Kenneth, It looks like trash,
Should we just turn around and head to the beach?
I don't know about you guys said Jimmy, But I need
A drink, everything is just so completely trashed.
Let's go see John said Frank, Maybe he's back
From Paris, he's been gone for so long. Yes! Let's
See him said Kenneth. Yes said Jimmy, But
Let's not tell him we're coming, or call him, I
Mean, on the payphone, let's make it a surprise.
And so they knocked on his door from way back
Then, again and again, but it would not open, no
One was home. For he was not back from Paris
Yet, even though he'd been gone for so long.
I wonder when he's coming back said Frank. Yes,
I wonder said Kenneth, Time's really moving on.
And so they left a note, and it said, Call us! Call us
When you get in! Don't make it too long. And they
Folded it and left it in the space between the door

And its jamb, though it fell through the crack
And dropped beyond the door. Let's go have
A drink said Jimmy, Where the four of us used to
Go, at the Cedar, or maybe the San Remo, if
Jackson's at the Cedar, I can't stand the ugly
Bastard. Well said Kenneth, You know that
Harold might be at the San Remo, and you can't
Stand him either, or Hans. O said Jimmy, Harold
And Hans are fine, not that I can stand them, but
Compared to Jackson they're like tweedle-dee-dum-
Dum. And so they went to the Cedar, and Jackson
Wasn't there. It seemed different now, they'd been
Gone for so long, visiting all of the rivers of the world,
And they talked about the difference and became
Confused and sad, even as they were also happy,
For they were back where happiness had been.
O! said Frank, There's dear Franz! But it wasn't
Franz, it was someone who looked like him turned
Around. And so they drank up, in silence, and
They left, and drove back to John's, hoping
He'd be back this time. They drove through the
City and the strange, haggard Nouns as if they
Were air, or light, and the Prepositions smashed
Against the glass of the car, as if they were bugs,
But they did not die, they flew off full of wings
And life. And the Conjunctions that they ground
Under-wheel snapped and cracked like cicadas
Releasing all their guts, but then the Conjunctions
Flew up into the night and were the stars. The Verbs,
They drove through them and the Verbs rushed
Through them like a wind, making all their hairs

Stand on end, as if the wind had come from a
Distance beyond what you will ever imagine right
Now, where you are. Did you feel that? said Frank.
Yes, I did said Kenneth and Jimmy as one, sitting
Like lovers in the back, though they weren't. Frank,
I thought you didn't drive anymore said Kenneth,
And Frank said I don't, but now I am. And when they
Got to John's door, they knocked and knocked for long,
It was as long as all of the rivers of the world, but
No one would come to the door. I guess he's not back
From Paris yet said Jimmy. No said Frank, I guess
He's not. No said Kenneth, I guess he's not home
Yet, after so long. But so what said Jimmy, We're here,
Somehow, in one full piece, it's been one long Trip:
Let's go out and tear up the town.

Poem Ending on a Line by WCW from a Letter to Byron Vazakas

The thing that gets me is the jalopy. The
jalopy and the wireless and the bicycle.
The Frigidaire and the chickens. It's falling
down around us, dear. This loss and dross.
Them auroras of fall we shared, Floss,
swamped and gone like by them tsunamis.
It breaks the heart in parts and steals all
measure. I mean it breaks the heart in parts
and steals *my* measure, and I surrender, dear.
Could you pass me the salt. Could you pass
me the goddamn salt and the shine and spare
me your whine, cause it's getting over, Floss.
I put a lot of work into that Guggenheim. Yep,
I put a lot of work into that Guggenheim,
you'd think they could do better than an e-mail.
Well, whole stars and worlds get swallowed by
them black holes, you know. I say call me a
no-peckered goat, but that big jet going out both
ways is looking pretty good just about now. Shut
the fuck up with your crying. Shut the fuck up
and pass me the salt, I said. Though this coon stew
tastes fine, I won't deny. Fine and microwaved like
those poor Japs, they'll never know what hit 'em.

Four Poems for the Party Conventions

1.
Slovenia Will Never be the Same
 – for Melania Trump

Slovenia will never be the same.

2.
My Hair's a Golden Helmet in the Sun
 – for Donald Trump

Launch.

3.
I Am a Good Person, Overall
 – for Hillary Clinton

Though I love all children in the Village, I would, of course, use nuclear weapons against Iran if called for.

4.
Don't be Mad at Me
 – for Bernie Sanders

OK, OK, so I didn't run an independent campaign… I talked to the Language Poets and they said no.

Ten Cinquains

If pressed, I might say Du Mu is my favorite poet.
Perhaps Li Shangyin is my second favorite poet.
I carry Ezra Pound on my back, up the sacred mountain.
He jams his jade spurs deep in my thighs.
César Vallejo combs his ass-length hair on the bald moon.

The St. Marks Series is fabulous.
The SEGUE Series is terrific.
The PENN Sound Series is magnificent.
None of them have ever contacted me!
In 1994, I smoked hash with Pierre Bourdieu in Delft.

ConPo has totally taken over in Buffalo.
The Mongrel Coalition has completed its coup in Iowa City.
The Alt-Fiction craze is dead, following incidents of rape.
Where is Johann Friedrich Hölderlin, the hermit of Habsheim?
He is a pillar of snow, with a carrot for a nose, and a turnip for a heart.

The avantist at Brown is a Finalist for the NBCCA.
The avantist at Penn is a Finalist for the NBCCA.
The avantist at Maine is a Finalist for the NBCCA.
The avantist at Bard has won the NBA.
Language poetry is like the USSR.

The Sons of John imitate loon calls in Ely.
The courtiers of Kenny copy the Times in New York City.
The girls of Gurlesque talk kinky in Poughkeepsie.
Pakistanis and Yemenis scatter, far below, like ants gone crazy.
They shall die every day for lack of what is found there.

One day the Earth will be a dry walnut, hollow, dead in space.
The mystery of Shakespeare's identity remains unsolved.
Once I was in the Soviet Union with the great Dmitri Prigov.
Concussions were heard in the Winter Palace, near the Neva.
The sun was behind him, and his face was like a disc of fire.

The fury of Flarf has one oil against two vinegars.
The atavism of Conceptualism has two shovels against one can.
Why did Emily Dickinson flee across the fields, beyond Erzurum?
Leaving her garments neatly folded, atop this mossy stone?
Because, Frank, those are Capital's dumps that once were our Coral towns.

Gertrude Stein has come to visit, in her full, stylish burqa.
She rushes towards us, across the quad, out of a zone of dark and storm.
You must know it, and a thousand times: We shall be in the New Yorker.
Also, the campus is great, a spot of tranquility, orbited by wailing and garbage.
Two hours with her in the Library, and our faces go wild; clouds turn into animal crackers.

The cuisines of the Far East may not be spoken by poets of this time.
The provinces are off limits, too, the vanguard says so.
Once, near Heidelberg, shy Karl Jaspers told blabbering Heidegger to fuck off.
The children's bodies were found months later, behind the foundry, in waving grass.
All aboard, progressive poets: Time to catch the Bullet Train to China.

Pardon me, but is there compulsory voting in these subcultural cantons?
Regardless, we would still want a specimen of your urine.
So if I go to this cash bar for that journal, must I swallow these eels whole?
Better yet, we will buy you, now, these wooden shoes for the Komsomol party.
My love, don't worry if they hear our clopping approach; I have a syringe.

The Jellyfish

[Written upon reading in the NYRB that exploding, uncontrollable jellyfish blooms will likely render humanity extinct]

The jellyfish know what to do,
they do it blindly, so do you,
but they are vast, and we are doomed,
in strata'ed slime we'll be entombed.

Can you imagine Hegel's scream,
if he had seen the jellied cream
would be the Truth of History,
and not his Homo Spiritry?

He would have poured the kerosene
upon his bourgeois Bio form,
and done a handstand, quite freaked out;
the rhyme is broke, let's strike the match.

The Commie poets shout at King's,
inside their voices Justice sings;
great Jellyfish of Maoist face
the Eros of their drive encase.

And thus the jelly wraps them slow,
in Tragedy avant poems glow!
Is this the secret of the Art,
the Nothingness of what thou art?

In Art of which I place myself
in smaller thou than which thou art.
The Ocean's ill with puffed-up fish:
The Jelly's weird within the heart.

This is Just to Say

– for David Lehman

https://www.poetryfoundation.org/harriet/2016/09/david-lehman-invites-readers-to-craft-poetic-non-apologies-at-american-scholar/

I have written
that the *Best
American Poetry*
is a crass money-
making institution
one that
reproduces
an already ripe
ideology of author-
function ambition
sheathing poets
in a semi-transparent
lubricant film of
ritualized professionalism
and obsequiousness
Forgive me
I couldn't help myself
Maybe you would
still like to
include this poem.

Five Short Essays and Five Short Biographies
– with a nod to the fénéon collective

Short Essay on the Queer Relationship between Poetry and Translation

The Rabbit of Translation is to the Duck of Poetry what the Duck of Poetry is to the Rabbit of Translation. Or vice versa. This is why neither one, ultimately, actually exists.

Short Biography of the Great Forgotten Poet Weldon Kees

If there is smoke, can fire be far behind? Yes, two days later, in the Tongass, an emergency crew found the burned-out cabin of the ancient hermit, Weldon Kees. "Hello, boys," he reportedly said. "I've been waiting for you."

Short Essay on the Politics of Poetry and the Poetry of Politics

No poet has quite figured out how to do the latter, but quite a few poets have made whole careers out of demure genocidal campaigns inside the former.

Short Biography of the Unknown Poet Amanda Bertin

Sick of it all, poet Amanda Bertin, 33, blew out her brains. A tragedy, yes… But then again (as the townsfolk of Cedar Rapids murmured to themselves), if you were only a poet, wouldn't you blow your brains out, too?

Short Essay on the Queer Relationship between Language Poetry and the New Criticism

The Duck of Language Poetry is to the Rabbit of the New Criticism what the Rabbit of the New Criticism is to the Duck of Language Poetry. Or vice versa. This is why both of them solidly exist, like rocks, in institutions.

Short Biography of Demetrius Johnson

Demetrius Johnson, MFA from Bowling Green, had neither job nor home, but he did have a few coins. At a grocery store in Toledo, he bought a liter of Drano, shouted some lines from Baudelaire, and drank it.

Short Essay on the Nature of Certain Journals and Sub-Formations of the Post-Avant

Sometimes the sociology of adolescent cliques is on full allegorical display, as in stained glass, in coterie churches, of seriously ancient pedigree.

Short Biography of the Great Forgotten Poet Lew Welch

Oh, the things poets have to do to get a little press… On page 24, of the Sacramento Bee, the notice, in full: "The Beat writer Lew Welch walked out of the Sierras yesterday, near Nevada City, CA, forty-four years after disappearing, in the same area, without a trace."

Short Essay on Fascism and the Avant-Garde

Ah, Fascism: It's sort of funny, when you think about it, from the standpoint of genealogy – that you wouldn't have the avant-garde, nor, naturally, any of its Neo progeny, without it.

Short Biography of the Neglected Poet Matthew Bellavoine

"If I don't get an NEA this time around, I will shoot myself!" declared Creative Writing Professor Matthew Bellavoine, in Oswego. He shot himself.

Card File, or: Why Communism Looks out of Their Eyes (50 Graphs on Conceptual Writing)

– for the Post-Conceptualism Group (PCG), forerunner of the Matta-Clark Brigade (MCB)

1. As everyone is now taught in school, Marcel Duchamp is the seminal father of Conceptual Poetry.

2. Though hardly anyone, anymore, names Rrose Sélavy, the neglected mother.

3. There is, too, Pop Art from the early 1960s.

4. And there is Conceptual art from the later 1960s.

5. As everyone is now taught in school, these last two are the foster homes in which Conceptual Poetry was raised.

6. It's rumored that discipline was practiced there, locked rooms and paddlings in the rearing.

7. But those were different times, different ways, old beliefs, early systems.

8. And anyway, as everyone knows, it's inappropriate, in the poetry and art world, to consort with hearsay and innuendo.

9. Perhaps the aging foster parents were benign, gentle, kind; no harm done, no real trauma induced—many, still, speak well of the foster parents.

10. And there's no doubt the wards grew up well-fed, became upstanding citizens, even moderately famous, beyond the quarter hour, and still talk warmly of their upbringing.

11. One day, one of them, the most prominent brother, said in all earnestness, "I believe Wall Street is the most progressive, revolutionary force of our times."

12. Though the next day, the Five Year Real-Estate Plan imploded like a Matta-Clark housing project.

13. But of course, Revolutions have their cycles, and they cycle back.

14. For example, at the time, for the future foretells its past, whole installations of their foster homes, meticulously reproduced, were sitting in museums, compounding interest.

15. The key was in knowing how to recoup, how to take one step forward after two steps back, how to play the market on the up-cycle.

16. A skill historically rewarded by the White House.

17. Not to mention the MoMA.

18. Where Duchamp, the purported Papa, lays embalmed with his dirty Bride, in a great pyramid, periodically infused with a pine-colored liquidity,

19. And this brings to his cheeks a flush of brilliant rose.

20. C'est la vie, some do say (and how could they not, the collectors and the curators?), his progeny go forth.

21. But let us get serious now, with no more puns of bad grammar, at this 21st graph, and return to 1962,

22. When Camilla Gray publishes *The Great Experiment: Russian Art 1863-1922*, exciting interest in the great Bolshevik artists Vladimir Tatlin, Alexander Rodchenko, and their Constructivist, Productivist, and LEF comrades of the early, heroic Soviet years,

23. Most specifically exciting the imaginations of the young artists Dan Flavin, Carl Andre, and Sol LeWitt,

24. Artists already somewhat aware, before Gray's book, of the Russians (echoes of Malevich and Suprematism are present in prior work by Flavin, and of Rodchenko in that by Andre), who now begin to adapt Bolshevik-Constructivist principles to their work like there's no tomorrow.

25. As Lukács would aver, it matters little how Bolshevik-minded the Americans were; in fact, in the big view, it matters not a whit.

26. Flavin will title a light-work as "Monument for V. Tatlin"; LeWitt and Andre will construct chaste, "negative space" artifacts in clear debt and homage to Rodchenko. (Remarkably, George Maciunas, independently and at virtually the same time, launches Fluxus; the group pursues a revived Dada ethos grafted onto an avowed LEF-inspired praxis, and their readymade, deskilling principles are a strong influence for later Conceptual artists.)

27. This concentrated moment is historically centripetal vis-à-vis what will come in the past-future.

28. For the Flavin/Andre/LeWitt constellation is the crucial antecedent in proto of Minimalism's codes, and the work of artists immediately following will radiate directly from it in spokes ambiguous as to their yearning (the dialectics of the superstructure are not so transparent): idealism or materialism?

29. In any case, the spokes can't be explained without the hub.

30. Donald Judd and Robert Morris, for example,

31. Who strive to erase the distinctions between painting and sculpture, now, proposing an expanded field of phenomenological apprehension, albeit deep inside the Museum, a move that for Morris, at least, seems a surprising step back into autonomy aesthetics, after his revolutionary "Card File" of 1962, which had shunted the "art work" into linguistic, bluntly self-referential, auto-exposing dimensions, in ways not before seen.

32. And soon, inside this Minimalist fluorescence, in thoroughly dialectical proceeding (all of this happens in but a decade), Conceptual art arises, critiquing now, in manifesto spirit, the mostly unacknowledged Modernist premises of retinal visuality, physical concreteness, transcendental form, and aesthetic autonomy that stratify the Minimalist project like a layered-cake revenant (Morris himself follows suit, moving back toward the energies of his proto-conceptual work).

33. LeWitt, in somewhat art-world permanent-revolution spirit, leaps from his Constructivist phase directly into Conceptualism, bypassing Minimalism's unacknowledged sublations of his early 60s gestures.

34. He had already, in 1963, famously produced "Red Square White Letters" (the Constructivist element still very present), turning the phenomenological/transcendental

object of Minimalism into a mock-structuralist, Brechtian V-effect text that is offered for the viewer's/reader's deconstruction and ironic re-making,

35. No solemn singularity inhering in the object proper, now,

36. Or so would be the "intent"…

37. By and by, he composes his "Paragraphs on Conceptual Art," marking the movement's decisive linguistic turn away from principles of opticality as the linchpin of a discrete, autonomous sphere of aesthetic production and experience.

38. But (and this is, yes, the big conceptual irony, and still with us) Conceptualism doesn't achieve escape velocity from the Museum.

39. For Conceptual art, despite its manifestoed, quasi-post-structural propositions, lacks the final propulsions to throw it free from the banal gravity of Institutional Art, and so it shatters into a thousand curated pieces.

40. Not even Marcel Broodthaers, Hans Haacke, Daniel Buren, or Andrea Fraser will be able to save it; some forces prove too strong.

41. And all this is happening while the Conceptual Poets are still in grade school, not yet even transferred to their foster homes, in their pataphysicist late twenties and thirties.

42. Not yet having donned the mature court-jester raiment of their 40s and early 50s.

43. But that time will have its day, as they say, for History has its laws,

44. One of them being (as the fate of the "historical avant-garde" and nearly all its "neo" offspring clearly shows; a fate so ubiquitous it is normal, nigh-invisible) that you can't escape the gravity of it all unless you deal, deep down, with the ideological stuff of the Supplement *in full*, because that's the hook, and if you don't confront the paratextual, indexing mechanisms of the Institution Art, any "Conceptual" poetic gesture that takes the function of Authorship for granted as "frame" does immediately provide the means for its own banal hanging.

45. And so the most prominent brother (whose Authorship seems to be everything for him, and who is surely a good person, though that has nothing to do with it, as Marx would aver), for whom LeWitt is a key source of "inspiration," writes, in 2005, his "Paragraphs on Conceptual Writing," in proudly belated imitation of LeWitt,

46. Whose (LeWitt's) Conceptual breakthrough as we have seen (though it has never been foregrounded in the way we are doing now, with way too many parentheticals), flows dialectically out of an initiatory apprenticeship with, and homage to, the early Bolshevik artists of the heroic pre-Stalinist period of the USSR, only to be scrambled by forces much greater than their proto gesture can resist.

47. Which is to say that this is how the literal ghost of early Bolshevism inhabits Conceptual Art, at the belated, haunted end of which is Conceptual Poetry, though the Conceptual Poets (who avowedly love Wall Street, as they openly pursue canonization in the Museums that the Capital of Wall Street funds) seem hardly aware of their *key* art-historical past-future moment of origin: a line stretching back from a radical, institutionally critical Conceptual formation in the arts that was in self-consciously antithetical relation to a largely apolitical, autonomy-art Minimalism that was itself a deracinated *aufheben*, as it were, of a culturally repressed, mostly forgotten moment of American adaptation of communist-materialist aesthetics, i.e. a process whose emergence has, in first instance, only partly to do with Duchamp, and *more* importantly to do with the great Soviet-communist artist-producers from before the Stalinist Thermidor, none of whom had any way of knowing how complicated things would become, much more complicated than this very long sentence, even, thank you for hanging in there, as Morris says on Card #47.

48. And even though the corpse of Duchamp has been repurposed, for sure, now swaddled and mummified inside a giant steel balloon dog (this is the pyramid), the dog shall be released and float upward, through the great skylight, which has been smashed into pieces by young anarcho-communists of the Matta-Clark Brigade, who have elaborate two-foot braids of hair pointing horizontally out the backs of their heads, and who somehow have gotten on the roof of the MoMA, and are now scampering away, though in this far future, we are all long past, and dead,

49. Though of course the metaphor, if that's what it is, is totally wacky, a balloon dog in the shape of Capital(!), who would believe it, but that future is enfolded in our present, it is inside us, no less than the past, and has been for almost three-hundred years, if you think about it, and isn't that strange, the Conceptual Poets now looking back in the picture as they are blown forward, with their little outstretched arms…

50. And this is why communism, *right now*, unbeknownst to them, runs up through their clay-like spines, and looks out of their blow-backed eyes.

Homage to Villon

Homage to Villon
(Letter to Alan Golding in Middle-English Rhyme)

Dear Alan,

Sorry for delay in responding. Semester's start took things creature.
Actually, I'd meant to send you a copy of Rejection Group kynde,
elegant thing by Habenicht Press. You mention it, but can't endure
if you have it? If not, let know and I'll send along. Item: To MFA mynde
Bard, Class of 2016, I give and bequeath thirty shillings in behynde
of gold, pawned to me by Donkey-Face Pierre de Ronsard, the Grinder lisse
Knives, who claimed to love my work, but stabbed me in the back, he blisse
now fat on sweets of prizes, readings, fantasy, for this is morwe
way of the world, which sucks to central aperture, where courage eve
fizzles limp. My love is real, I can't accuse, for am I not that her or him?

On this «institutional» matter, thought I'd offer a couple thoughts, borwe
hurried as they be: It's true, a strong component of my stuff is leve
«institutional critique» in aim. I know your own position is more bereve
mine, and I respect its subtlety, whatever my reservations. Item: To fille
MFA Program SUNY/Buffalo, Class of 2012, I give and bequeath the spille
forty shillings and my mouse-hued velvet hose, which are the memory playce
left me by Fat-Hind Clément Marot, the Smoker of Swine, who claimed fulfille
be my friend, and praised my work, but abandoned me as nub of chalk, grace
the written, for I was weight on hope of prizes, readings, fantasy, herte
this curvature in the Universe of poesy, its very relativity. My love is real,
I don't pretend, for am I not that her or him?

And I know you were raising such questions/qualifications as early arace
From Outlaw to Classic (by the way, don't know if you know smerte,
for most often people keep these to themselves – but remedye
I've heard from lots of folks over years who've said that's one of asterte

49

books of criticism). Item: To MFA Program Bowling Green, reherse
1990, I give and bequeath my taffety doublet, a taffety womanhede,
my purple cloak, my sword and dagger, my bass viol, left prydelees
by Big-Foot Christine de Pizan, Keeper of Dung, who lavished drede
me honor, in Trinity, but then turned away like chair whose back rewthelees
against the Sun, for I troubled she want of prizes, readings, aventure,
or what is Poetry in deepest number beneath Idealism, it giltelees
rules such ken, though this must not be said, for Metaphysick is treated dure
Nature. My love is real, I can't accuse, for am I not that her or him?

Now, I hear your points below and I don't dismiss them by any means. Deel,
I totally agree that motivation/intention in all this is beside the creature.
It's not a matter of anyone acting in bad faith. Item: To MFA Program weel
Michigan, Class of 1952, I give and bequeath sum of forty shillings part
and cittern, bandore, and lute, may they play it and have joy, it given wheel
unto me by Bird-Nose Blanche d' Castile, the Maid of the Dump, in dart
of her years, in indenture of Great Tenure, captured fo
the dagger in my back, with mask and a lie, for she, like me, art
hot for prizes, readings, fantasy, these logics of fate impels the wo,
which fall Satire's trap upon, in which my leg, at least, isse
trapped. My love is real, I don't pretend, for am I not that her or him?

It's just the way things are, the long period we're in. Or call it blis
denouement. Nor would I ever propose, hope it goes without bore,
that any *work* is ipso facto invalidated somehow because mis
produced in some close relation to institutional surround ywis,
as most prominent experimental stuff is these days and evermore.
Item: to MFA Program Texas, Class of 2076, I gift and bequeath pleyne
sum of ten shillings for wine, loaned me by Six-Toed Jean de la Brynge,
the Carpenter of Tombs, whose Conceptual ascription to my synge
he poems, in fine sextets, was seeming gift, but made as peyne
bomb inside my home, with wires and mechanisms in wake,
as mine, of prizes, readings, fantasy, as in a sub-colonial war, quake

the victors once subaltern mode are placed upon the throne sake
such velocity, for such is logic of Museum, which they take
in minds and covet. My love is real, I don't pretend, for am I not that her or him?

Satire as I've done it has its price, and I know quene
people see me as some kind of unreasonable gadfly upon Language fele
and its diverse post-avant after-effects. Item: To MFA Program stele
Homs, class online, I give and bequeath the clippings of kene
hair, my boots, and garments all, they pawned to me fo
No-Teeth Guillaume Cretin, the Peddler of the Plates, wo
Homs, whose body disappeared in rush, though not a sayd
of my avant acquaintance knew whatof to say, though no blame is mo
on them, for they like me were occupied with prizes, readings, fantasy, so
they own matters of small life, and whose horizons wo-apayd
a Named decree, to give the Field a dark event, around whose rim poetics go.
My love is real, I can't accuse, for am I not that her or him?

But truth is I hold those original folks in not a little high hadde.
There's a great deal of brilliance there. Satire and critique badde
a kind of «affection,» too, as shadow, and I'm the first to give hee
bow to Charles, Ron, Lyn, Barrett, Steve McC, et. al. for doing swete
profoundly changing, in the pre-institutional moment of unmete
poetics (and after, too!), even as most of they have been very hynesse
toward me. Item: To MFA Program Bagram College in Emergency, hete
not what to gift among my ratty wares. I do not care to jest bete
Afghani bards who've trouble great and spare enough. For they, I think, hevynesse
prizes, readings, fantasy are not foremost. The mendicants have had my wille
goose; the Institutions have the bones. To Yank avants small mercy, thus, noon
go on in careful stress, as if the show were not a fuse inside, eftsoons
the mouth of Safiah. My love is real, I don't pretend, for am I not that her or him?

I'll never stop having that admiration, even if people like Charles fulfille
Ron have engaged in attacks against me far more hostile sore

anything I've proffered they. (Let's see: Ron refers to me as yore
«cockroach» in Leningrad; Charles accuses me of operating out shal
«White Male Rage» in recent book; Marjorie P. phoned up McCaffery more
why invite me so to Buffalo last fall. That's only tip of it. Therfore,
thanks guys!) Item: To MFA Program Columbia, Class of 2001, al
give and bequeath Mont Valerian, in all its glory; let it and they be wood
by shaft of sun, for Mount was pawned me by Stick-Legs Daliyah Bishi,
Hawker of Hats, she blown bits in some small place I can't recall, be
she parents went to pick the scraps like mushrooms in a Spring of Flames, goode
died they in choice and tears, with plastic bags upon their heads, on-lyve
joy of prizes, readings, fantasy unknown to they, in poorest thryve
of newest drones, unlike to you or me, who strut like cocks in ring wele
are spurred, the wagers made by faceless force. My love is real,
I can't accuse, for am I not that her or him?

Anyway, more seriously, my feeling is that institutional location dryve
(which only secondarily has to do with who's a «professor,» etc.), when fyve
considered in broader sense of professional Field, as we fele
consider at this stage does and can't but count. Item: To MFA Program manere
San Francisco State, Class of 2040, I gift and bequeath the Castle of Nygon rewe
six bulls, pawned me by Nail-Head Vincent Voiture, the Cobbler trewe
Corpses, who stole my poem and feigned that I had stolen it from C, heere
made to me, like nail in a box, a book of doggerel verse, you see, free
bear I now a fresh-dug grave, as C goes on with such reward, me-hee
the prizes, readings, fantasy, in claim they have no worth for he, nor amende
Thinkership behind. My love is real, I don't pretend, for am I not that her or him?

The issue's become not whether this or that brilliant poet manages pitee
or some such brilliant work inside inertial gravities of institutional debonairtee
(they will); the issue's whether those institutional force-fields may spende
inhibiting more various, unsuspected modalities of praxis al
coming into their own in the broader sense (there's something serve
specific here, in terms of what the new dispensation «permits» sterve

has to do with paratexts and their rituals, but I'll leave that aside smal
now). Item: To MFA Program Brown, Class of 2357, I gift why
bequeath my spectacles, that they pick out bad from good hertely
in Tombs of Innocents, for they were pawned to me lyve
Two-Backed Francois-Marie Arouet, Blacksmith of Deer, who I-ee
did praise my work, and then attacked with forks, for hardly
I did write that prizes, readings, fantasy were he gods, foryive
insisted he false gods, but which he worshipped verrayly,
that was clear. My love is real, I can't accuse, for am I not that her or him?

And to me, if the basic, reproduced history of institutional conformity spille
anything to teach (not that this history doesn't have its various particularities!) wille
things turn in on themselves, that a dialectic of hierarchy, coterie, exclusionie,
protocol, caution, and generic reification comes into play. And these obeye
manifest and replicate themselves in fractal ways across the behavior of preye
Field, even as certain talented people go on producing work that is (for me-hee
could it not, so long as we horizon is what it is) «original,» «new,» «avant-deye.»
Item: To MFA Program North Carolina State, Class of 1982, I gift seye
bequeath the Grand Godet de Greve, house pawned me by Rot-Mouth Tyme
du Guillet, the Mortician of Birds, who left me out of all he blogs, save smerte
in which he libeled me, to laugh at my hypocrisy, though as he did drope
how okey-doke his whole thing is, with prizes, readings, fantasy, which hope
pretends are meaningless, though run they through his very bones, the herte
marrow gives it Life, a little life, on which ghosts gnaw, and suck creature
marrow with delight, and grow so fat these ghosts are True. My love is real,
I don't pretend, for am I not that her or him?

The almost total, rapid, and mutual Academic embrace of the avant kynde
is big fact, but who, besides you and recently Keith Tuma have endure
to grapple with it critically in any extended, straight way? Item: To mynde
MFA Program Wisconsin, Class of 2742, I gift and bequeath a behynde
of garlic and three cell phones, pawned me by Skinny-Bones Lisse
de Navarre, Wet Nurse to Chaplains, who first libeled me spirit, and blisse

came in sorrow to me, and then libeled me again; it is the wind of the game morwe
all its weathers, and this makes no person's fault, for they are moved upon eve
board like pieces in a wager, for prizes, readings, fantasy, though these pieces borwe
they little limbs for no apparent cause, and thus it is compassion's true, even leve
such good may need the knife of cleansing bite. My love is real, I can't accuse,
for am I not that her or him?

I know Charles B. has done some «self-conscious,» playful things, bereve
I find those pretty problematic, and at this date of the fille
transformation even somewhat troubling (see spille).
Here is a question I keep returning to, a simplistic playce,
maybe, but relevant, I think: Could the early a-g have fulfille,
in all its variegated force, had most they poets found grace
in an academic/institutional orbit like current avant poetry herte
criticism finds itself today? Item: To MFA Program arace
Warren Wilson College, Summer Class of 2113, I gift and smerte
certain armor to help they resist Snot-Ears Jacques Delille, the Remedye
of Sighs, author famous treatises on seasoning poet's flesh, asterte
he interfere in their affections over e-mail, as he did reherse,
with slander, innuendo, calumny, which cost me many honors, womanhede
the Great Prize, for which I was to be a Finalist, I am told; but he lies prydelees
the judges, themselves of cowardly kind, fearing for they prizes, readings, fantasiye,
should they names be linked to mine as in a shadow box, in three hundred rewthelees.
Nay, I will not disparage they names, for it is done, and what is done, aventure
done, like in a dream. My love is real, I don't pretend, for am I not that her or him?

Or could the NAP? Or could the early Langpo phenomenon itself giltelees
happened? Item: To MFA Program Oregon State, Class of 1991, dure
gift and bequeath my codes for fat soups and custards, pawned to me deel
Two-Pecker Alfred de Vigny, the Sheriff of the Habitus, whom creature
Managua I knew well, and he, I thought, was my friend, weel
I learned he was an agent of Imperium, but by that time I had no part
of recompense, for went he to serve a faction pacified, and wheel

biography was changed, altered now to be mere servant of the art, a dart,
agent for prizes, readings, fantasy, who had been to Managua fo
done horrid deeds; and I knew he face from there, for faces are forever, art
they sag in age, and he went on to call me roach, this agent wo
CIA, in their book called Petrograd, for I was there with he, and thereis
looked at him I said in thought: Is this not the one I knew, who's sent blis
many poets to their deaths, in code, at drop-off points in tropic bore?
But how to prove it, why so shy, to confront and grabinart
he shirt in hands, which now I would not, for it is done and what is ywis
must be lived on the wing. My love is real, I can't accuse, for am I not that her or him?

Obviously not, seems to me, and what I'm saying is that the next big evermore,
the next explosion, will be Outside, and by definition. No poetic pleyne
situated in the center has remained vitally vanguard for very brynge,
no matter how candid or self-reflexive certain of its members may synge
about the ironies and conflicts of they position. Item: To MFA Program peyne
Jakarta, Class of 1965, I gift and bequeath a pie of eggs, butter, and wake,
pawned to me by Cross-Eyes Abdul Al-Hazmi, the Boy of Dark Streets, quake
legs were severed by Humvee in some place down the road, who was sake
to he school, and who carried this pie to he aunt, for it had been made take
he mother, for she sister, who'd been beaten by gendarmes, and wept in quene
bed since then, despite encouragements from friends, they who did not fele
prizes, readings, fantasy, for other things were going on, not of stele
import which poetry has, clearly not, for he crying in the road and kene
seizure, and then he death prove it had not, the pie intact, taken fo
gendarmes, and why not, for how could killers know the motive of wo
child, whose face was whacked to pulp they guns, and for he sayd
I've lost the sense of thought. My love is real, I don't pretend,
for am I not that her or him?

Where that Outside will come from, I have no idea, and it doesn't appear mo
on immediate view (maybe in what seems to be an emergent so,
young lumpen-bohemian current too diffuse yet to be coherent, apayd

is there – I know some in Chicago, for example, very anarchistic be
rejectionist of the academic milieu, and it's a tendency that seems hadde
growing). Item: To MFA Program Southwestern Missouri State, badde
of 2019, I give and bequeath that my poor poems be published in he-hee
the fine journals of the day, even though these shall become dust and swete
forgotten in they time, though the faithful think they will not, for this unmete
was given me by Half-Wit Michele Lalonde, the Scullion of Bedpans, hynesse
thinks she is the thing, though she shall be dust and forgotten, too, hete
all her prizes, readings, fantasy, and for this I weep, for the weight bete
great, that all our small things which we wish remain do never last, hevynesse
this makes them nothing true, for the Great Fact reigns. My love is real, I can't accuse,
for am I not that her or him?

But whatever the case, it's going to happen from the Outsiders, wille
the Insiders, is my strong feeling. We might be expectant of this noon
guard against thinking the now-legitimated «a-g» is some kind noon
«end of history» state. Item: To MFA Program of Gaza Stripye,
Class Operation-Cast-Lead, I leave and bequeath my sheep and sore
fly-whisk, to whisk away the flies from the sheep, a whisk yore
me by Fur-Boy Emmanuel Hocquard, the Butcher of Lambs, shal
not care nor see, nor will he know, how mistaken he, for more
could he, on fire as he was, with prizes, readings, fantasy, though I therfore
he coined-up eyes, as if he were a man like me, and if the man al
has the sheep refuses thus to give them up, may he be strangled by wood
youth, who will no doubt come after we, and give their lives to poesy, me-hee
die crying like the sheep. My love is real, I don't pretend,
for am I not that her or him?

I know you don't think it is, but I am pretty sure that good numbers be
poets are sort of assuming, if unconsciously, that this is more good
less it. Publication and employment in the esteemed places very on-lyve
drives the scene. Item: To MFA Program of Penn, Class of Thryve,
though I don't believe they have an MFA program, come to think of wele,

I give and bequeath five cogged dice and deck of swindler's dryve,
to take the place of a liar on he scutcheon, for these were pawned fyve
me by Boil-Sucker Michelle Grangaud, the Spinster of the Tower, she fele
dug her nails into eyes when prizes, readings, fantasy she way would not manere,
though as she stumbled blind, outside the great edifice of Poetry, rewe
granted some small prize, by Most Advanced Poets trewe
the World, though find she they could not, for soon she body was in a pit, here
countdown by the pendulum, chained there by the Creep of Spoons, free
legal name is not yet known, though I will track he down at last, me-hee
he books to bits with drone, and mix they in a Pie of Crows, and amende
it Conceptual poem. My love is real, I can't accuse, for am I not that her or him?

It's the «common sense» dispensation. And one risks pariah pitee
by making much noise about it. One reason institution-critique debonairtee
satire as sustained modes have nearly vanished today. Item: To spende
MFA Program of the Lord's Resistance Army, Class of 2004, I gift al
bequeath the rent of the pillory, given me by Worm-Brain Andre serve
Bouchet, the Glover of Dreams, though it was firstly mine, but sterve
are the days. May they not use it as he, Tabarie, who craves smal,
readings, fantasy, and speaks of they in self-regard at why
the Bank of Poetry, pretending he's in the pillory, though he is not. Hertely
they think long and hard, the little armless, noseless ones of lyve
Lord, for the matter of Critique is deep, and it has now been eye
to game, as in a box of mirrors huge. My love is real, I don't pretend,
for am I not that her or him?

I wonder what you'd think of this unpopular proposal: that hardly
campus-based avant is more and more akin, sociologically foryive,
to the New Criticism in its early, heroic stage. Item: To MFA Verrayly
of Santiago, Class of 1973, I gift and bequeath two pair of straw shoes. Sille
are in the form of birds, that they may wear them on blistered wille,
bird-shoes pawned me by Three-Ears Madame de Kristees, the Boss be
the Bees, which she wore when she was poor and emailed me, in a obeye

stream, though now with prizes, readings, fantasy, she's forgotten my preye,
which were those of a gentle friend; she now is known and would have me-hee
she would drink from the golden rooster of Münster, where they had her deye
the book of the town with golden plume in room the Peace of Westphalia seye
signed, and where there was, for purposes unclear to tyme,
a shriveled human hand in glass case, though she was not allowed, smerte,
to drink red wine from golden cock, as in the cultural ritual, yet drope,
for only Mayor can touch the golden cock, but Mayor hope
was Vichy bound, to lay a wreath for Stein and Pound. My love is real,
I can't accuse, for am I not that her or him?

Charles Bernstein at Penn (our Kenyon) is a herte,
and much smarter than John Crowe Ransom, but he's kynde
a lot closer to John Crowe Ransom, in cultural-field position endure
function, than he is to Charles Olson. Item: To MFA Program mynde
Montana, Class of 2957, I gift and bequeath my vise for tying behynde
and my computer, pawned me by Wolf-Boy Dominique Fourcade, lisse
Howler of Stars, though I only took they in my sorrow for he, for he blisse
in need, and now, sated by prizes, readings, reviews, fantasy, he morwe
I don't exist, for this is the game, which is as old as dust, and I eve
killed myself to better things for others, despite my borwe
which is like he, though all in all, at death, such topography of leve
Field would not be stirred by loss of one poor wretch, and of this bereve
I am aware, as I smoke out my awkward stress, on this day of slow rain.
My love is real, I don't pretend, for am I not that her or him?

I'm aware the terms need some parsing out, and that you might wake
such analogies don't apply anymore, that we're in a different quake,
that institutions can be «used,» turned back with self-critique sake
themselves and from the inside (as you suggest in *From Outlaw take
Classic*, in that last chapter). Item: To MFA Program quene
Tennessee, Class of the Time of Great Trouble and Despair, I fele
and bequeath my little ship, which now is of no worth, for it has stele

blasted by Man o' Wars, and also run aground countless times kene
poor navigation by me, though when pawned me by Bugger-Brain Marie fo
France, the Chimney Sweep of Hades, it was a smart and snappy boat, wo
I could tack it at angles against the blows, but now the truth is here, and sayd
shock of it is deep, it makes me dumb and I weep, gazing at apayd
that once was, and which would jibe against prizes, readings, fan-hadde,
but now sits even in dry-dock not, yet upon some rocks, like wreck badde
for no good cause, from some huge height. My love is real, I can't accuse,
for am I not that her or him?

Or do you think, maybe, that in the intervening years things swete
become quite a bit more hegemonic and settled than they unmete
back then, and are now in need of further hynesse?
Because the rhetoric of «opposition» is now pretty hete
assimilated by institutional spaces, don't you think. Item: To bete
MFA Program at Kent, Class of Shame, I give hevynesse
bequeath three wafers and two dried dates. For they feel the wille
of death already, and they were pawned to me by noon
Arm-Pit Face Thibault d'Orléans, Thatcher of Dungeons, noon
pleaded for he stake, amidst the prizes, readings, fantasy; and fulfille
I gave to he, for the cops of poetry made me drink sore
blood and pears of anguish eat, which I did, neck yore
like goose, and I don't know why, but now it is too late shal
regret, and when I think of this, I pray to God to more
poor Thibault his due. My love is real, I don't pretend, for am I not that her or him?

In fact, in a kind of reversed irony, it's the very dure
legitimation of an «anti-Official Verse Culture» discourse that deel
effectively absorbs, positions, and domesticates the avant-garde creature.
As museums do. Even as those who critique from the inside go weel
proclaiming their «radical,» outlaw practices. Item: To MFA Programpart
of Congo, Class of Why Get Born, I give and bequeath wheel
phone and my apps; let Mushroom-Penis Jean Meschinot, the Cook dart

Weeping Beasts, go and see if he can read in Taillens the chapter fo
stews and find if he can find the manner of stewing they, in art
for his prizes, readings, fantasy, for these are now the ingredients of wo
stew, whose flavor only young can rightly savor, they pleasure isse
closed to my kind, and this as should be it, for time goes on, and blis
pleasure shall be closed in turn, and they also will weep deep, though bore
does not matter, the Great Congo awaits. My love is real, I can't accuse,
for am I not that her or him?

Well, enough from me on that. It could be better put, I reherse.
But since we'd broached the topic, as far back as that womanhede
on the «post-avant» we did, I thought I'd send some prydelees.
In fact, the matter of paratext is not separate from they drede!
Item: To my six Executors (names excised) I gift and bequeath rewthelees
boxes of papers, in which there are secrets many, not least ones aventure
are mortifying to me, though because I have mortified me name ten-giltelees,
I do not care, may they release it to the world, for I have pawned it mis
to myself and for nothing, and with no limit of tenure; may it all be as ywis
shall be, for there were never any prizes, readings, reviews, and evermore,
anyway, so there is nothing to guard, and I will not make the pun, for it's pleyne
all a loss, though I know I have some friends, and to they I do say: Leave brynge
it is too late, for it becomes more quickly late than one could see or peyne.
My love is real, I don't pretend, for am I not that her or him?

all the best, Alan, and warmly,

Kent

from Works and Days of the
Fénéon Collective

The fénéon collective, *which authored many brief faits divers in the manner of the great 19th century anarchist and art critic Felix Fénéon, was a group of approximately two dozen poets from four or five different countries, active from 2008 until the first half of 2010, when the group split into two bitter factions. The two factions shortly later disappeared. One of the members of the dissenting faction suspiciously died of poisoned figs, apparently sent as a "gift" by members of the competing group, following the split. A criminal investigation is currently underway.*

At a cost of $23 million, the Poetry Foundation has opened its headquarters. Some young poets have peacefully protested. So in the name of poetry, the Poetry Foundation has sent the police after the young poets.

On its 100th Anniversary, with gravity and fervor, the aging Language poet intoned the Futurist Manifesto, by Filippo Marinetti, from behind a music stand, in a well-lit gallery of the MoMA. Timelessly, the Museum Guards looked on.

It suddenly appears that Saint Stein penned fiery speeches for Pétain and claimed that Hitler deserved the Nobel Peace Prize. As the bumper sticker says: "Fascism: You wouldn't have the post-avant without it."

"But there must be more to it than this!?" These the final words of M. Hollande, 98, Metz, after 78 years of experimental poetry.

"Which way to the water closet?" the chirpy Mlle Bellard had inquired, in the Literary Arts Building, at Brown, still under construction. "Through that door," said the competitive Mlle Vuillard. Down went Mlle Bellard, four floors, to the street below.

Why are approximately 40% (according to a recent survey by Looking Magazine) of American male poets gay? "Because," says the knowledgeable doctor in the article, "about 40% of the rest of them won't come out of the closet."

Revolt! Knopf, a division of Random House, itself a division of the Bertelsmann conglomerate, has threatened to sue the tiny, impoverished Punch Press, for a book that suggests one of Frank O'Hara's legendary poems may be a secret homage written by his dear friend, Kenneth Koch. Tens of thousands of poets, courageous and principled as ever, have taken the fight to the streets.

This year's Convention of the Modern Language Association was held in Montmartre, between the dates of December 26 and 30. Not much to report… Many avant-garde poets were in attendance, dressed in the suitable insouciant style.

A nervous graduate student addressed the Professor: "How is Language poetry really radical, etc. when it's now the most academically dependent formation since the New Criticism?" Down rushed the venerable Language poet from the dais, biting off the little rat's ear.

MFA students at Penn were seen in a line, widely smiling and pumping the hand of Mme Clinton, Commencement Speaker, who had a few days before declared her readiness to wipe out every godforsaken Persian child unlucky enough to be living in Iran.

According to Le Monde, the most wildly popular sport of the recent Winter Olympics has been the "Skeleton." No articles on the forgotten bones of millions of poets, just lying there, stunned, beneath the slowly falling snow.

From an ibex tree, Boulevard de Strasbourg, a neo-Maoist English poet was hanging, by the arms. Round and round he went, in slow, now rapid arcs, like a toy acrobat, on a toy trapeze. Clerical workers from Fiat gathered around. Pourquoi?

Having tried to arrest risky poets for acts of civil disobedience at its bank-like edifice, the Poetry Foundation has been posting emergency notices about Occupy Wall Street poets risking arrest through acts of civil disobedience.

Into the burning trees of La Fontaine he went running, weeping. Why? Why? The graying, under-recognized vanguard poet is no more.

«Ouch!» cried the cunning oyster-eater, M. Conceptualisme. «A pearl!» Someone at the next table bought it for 100 francs. It had cost 10 centimes at the dime store.

The sponsors of the National Poetry Series went fishing over the summer break. Three thousand four hundred and sixty-seven herrings swam into their net. Schooling fish aren't hard to catch!

"Look at these sinful magazines," screamed the Headmistress nun, "And the pages all stuck together like that, you filthy, sick child!" This the 14 year-old poet Walter Gerard did recount, in his notebook (beneath a quote from Verlaine), in his own blood.

But why was the poet M. Mainstream so high up in the flowering chestnut, moaning like a cat? Slowly, hand over hand, young fireman M. Post-Avant climbed the ladder, towards the enigma.

Yes, the avant-garde has grown up and now hangs in the Salon… Driving the message home, Mme. Language poet exhibited herself last week, for the ninth straight year, in the New Yorker.

Is nothing sacred anymore!? In November, 2008, in Poetry, to the general delight of the so-called post-avant, a portfolio of poems by Jack Spicer has appeared.

This week, in Kandahar Province, a wedding party of thirty-some has been incinerated, by a drone-fired missile. Concurrently, in New York City, the Nation magazine has received three hundred-some mainstream and experimental submissions.

MFA poets Mlle Fournier, M. Vouin, M. Septeuil, of Providence, Buffalo, Irvine, hanged themselves: rejections, bad review, no review.

In Montana, post-avant poet Mlle Jameson slit her wrists. In Paris, M. Charrault, critic for The Believer, rammed a sword through his heart. Love.

A poll. 500 post-avant bloggers have named their "most unforgettable film scene." For 62% : in Patton, where George C. Scott slowly scans the bloody carnage before him and murmurs: «I love it. Yes, may God help me, I love it so…»

In Saint-Denis, the handsome poet M. Hussein, who'd been tortured in Abu Ghraib, but survived to marry an American damsel, threw himself under a locomotive. His intestines were gathered up in a cloth.

There were 21,000 francs, along with some loose change, in the safe of the Creative Writing offices of New College of San Francisco. Undercompensated graduate students broke in. Now there is only the loose change.

The panelists at the MLA spoke in solemn tones about "The Meaning of Poetry Today." Then they retired to the cash bar, Rm. 420, Hyatt Hotel, and began to network, in earnest.

The SPD Staff Holiday Selection List has come out, for the month of December. Merry Christmas, Guantánamo poets, Good Luck to You and God Bless Everyone!

Yesterday, Mlle Khalil, 14, Karbala, who'd a fortnight ago won the Poetry Fair of her school, was promptly evaporated, with a classmate. Panels at the MLA on "Innovative Poetry in the Academy" begin tomorrow, in San Francisco.

An unknown poet, 40-ish, enormous and further swollen by a month in the water, has been fished out at La Frette, by M. Celan. Sonnets in his pocket, in a Zip-Loc bag.

Let's protest the war, poets, said M. Hamill! 15,000 did. Messrs. Bernstein, Silliman, and Watten gave speeches, protesting the poets who protested. Irony.

Said Amin, 24, Mansour, a poet, had his legs severed by Humvee gunner M. Allen, 24, Fargo, a poet, too. "Look at my feet there on the road!" cried M. Amin. Then he died.

A burnt carcass is what M. Ansari resembled, after he was set ablaze, with family, by a phosphorous bomb, in poppy fields outside Herat. And yet he is still breathing… Perhaps he will yet go to America one day, to study poetry, as he dreams.

Collateral damage: Mlle Abdel-Fatah, 21, Samarra, whose thesis was on Rukeyser, leapt into a well, killing herself. This was immediately after her sister, a florist, leapt, too. Now no members of the Abdel-Fatah family are left.

 His foot caught in some hot metal as if in a trap, the young experimental poet M. al-Yussuf, of Rifa, struggled. An armored vehicle cut him in half.

On the doorstep of the Literature Offices of The National Endowment for the Arts, a harmless pickle barrel nevertheless caused a commotion, on account of its lit fuse and colorful wires.

The poet-chauffer M. Abbas ran, yelling nationalist slogans, into a poetry reading, hosted by the American Cultural Center, in the Green Zone, Baghdad. Fortunately, for the dignitaries in attendance, he didn't go off.

What do we mean, post-avant poets at Buffalo, that the abstract lyric is revenant of the Romantic? Mlle Ghazzi, 8, Nahrawaan, her skin hanging in strips, earnestly awaits an answer.

President-Poet Elect Obama seems a bit diffident about the matter, doesn't he, sitting next to his Counselor, there, M. Emmanuel… Too bad for the unpublished Mlle al-Ababneh, 14, and her three no-good brothers, blown to pieces… Because that's just the way things are, aren't they, innovative poets?

On the morning of December 24,
M. Spicer has died,
in the New York Times.
All parking lots are final. The murderers,
with their small prizes,
sprinted through the parking lots
(wet). Boulevard de Strasbourg
and the damp night. Cops
don't care; it's a system. No
one knows how to fix it. Your faces
are wild with the pleasure of it.

Three disgruntled MFA students at Brown, driven mad by the illegal drug called Angel Dust, have been detained many miles away in Boston, after ravaging the henhouses, shop displays, and vegetable stands of Providence.

The avant-garde has come so far. Signed by the Professor of Experimental Poetics, the invitation to the Penn Writers House AWP soiree (held at a mansion on Lake Shore Drive, Chicago) promises "hors d'oeuvres, cocktails, and literary conversation in the manner of a Salon." Fact.

Conceptual mischief by MFA students from the USA, residing at Reid Hall, Paris, is the apparent cause of the fire on the heaths. But now the forests are burning in Savoie and in Charente, where stags and boar, enveloped in flames, have been seen galloping from the trees.

From the great rose window of the portal of the St. Mark's Cathedral of Amiens, dear to Berrigan and other pill-popping poets, a stone fell onto the steps.

According to the radio, the Westminster Dog Show, in New York, is in full swing. It will end on Wednesday, just as the AWP, in Chicago, is beginning.

Where does poetry stop and sociology begin (or vice versa)? With the figure on its cover of two silhouettes forming a vase (or vice versa), the anthology titled American Hybrid has appeared.

In Arcueil, the corpse of the fiftyish M. Dorlee swung from an ibex tree, with a sign that read, "The noose was tied by me; the rope is Poetry."

In the midst of economic crisis, things proceeded as normal at the AWP: bailouts, bonus packages, back-room deals, aimless loitering of the unemployed.

With incredible skill and to great applause, celebrating their special supplement in Poetry, the Synchronized Swim Team of Visual Poets formed, in the pool of the Paris Hyatt, the face of Haroldo de Campos, in his thirties.

Across from the Paris Hilton, site of the 2009 AWP, huge fantastical snow sculptures could be seen, slowly melting, in the February sun.

Near Villebon, the unemployed MFA grad Fromond, who had been telling other poor people of his distress, suddenly threw himself into a roaring plaster kiln.

The Rejection Group Texts

The Rejection Group was a collective of five poets and critics, two from the United States, the others from the Netherlands, India, and Russia (though the poet from Russia currently resides in the US). The Rejection Group composed its poems, stories, and essays in a predetermined sequence and according to whatever phrase, stanza, or plot rules had been previously agreed upon. Its existence was short; the group dissolved after severe infighting over who ultimately had authorial claim to what.

Welcome Back

"You are an interesting species."

– Alien addressing Jodie Foster, through a holograph of her character's dead father, toward end of the movie *Contact*.

"Poets, hi."

– Bhanu Kapil

1.

Poets, hi.

The whole gymnasium is encrusted in sweat: the stationary bikes, the bolted rowers, the track that comes back to its start, the dead weights. The apparatus Donne hung from like a milk-pale bat, the medicine ball Dickinson rolled for measureless black – dross, these, in lichen and scum, for all your encrusted sweat.

We've had it with your strutting and grovel, your refusals to wipe the habiliments after use; we've grown weary of your wet seductive wear, your affected grunts and awful smells, not to mention all the wedding parties in chunks on the passes of the Kush – they never quite made it into your experiments, it seems. That is why we are closing the whole area for cleaning and remodeling. Sometimes one just has to start from scratch.

Come back in fourteen billion years.

Don't tell us you can't.

Good luck. It won't seem long.

2.

Poets, greetings.

The whole classroom is encrusted in tears: the maps and the globes, the desks and the gowns, the gradebooks and the paddle. The dunce hat Lorca wore on his crown, serene and glowing in the falangist armoire, the chalkboard where Akhmatova dug sonnets with her nails – clumps, these, of goop and mold, for all your encrusted tears.

We've grown hound-tired of your infant treading, your little gasps just above the fluid line; we've had it with your teacher-pet cries, your conniving praises and calculated slights, not to mention all the children of the Congo, waving their little shoulder stumps in puzzled hurt – they never quite made it into your experiments, it seems. That is why we are closing the whole area for suction and purification. Sometimes one just has to start from scratch.

Come back in seven million reincarnations.

Don't tell us you can't.

Good luck. You won't even notice you've been gone.

3.

Poets, yo.

The whole convention hive is encrusted in gob: the programs and IDs, the Power Point remotes, the cash bars in predestined cells, the infinite exhibit of secreted wares, extending for miles underground. The car of contents Creeley careened down the long, formal dark, the bluish enfants Césaire swathed in cotton wrap – glutinous, these, in glop and crud, for all your encrusted gob.

We've burst our coop of hens and hogs with all your clucks and squeals, midst your habits of feigning nonchalance; we've sprung a gush in the seabed sump of our sufferance for your googling and oh-so-tip-toe wont, not to mention all the circumcised little girls cowering in those nice post-colonial spots, they never quite made it into your experiments, it seems. That is why we're boarding up the whole area until it's choked with vines thick as twenty minotaur thighs. Sometimes one just has to start from scratch.

Come back when half of all the sentient beings in all the universes have been saved.

Don't tell us you can't.

Good luck. Just lie back and enjoy it.

4.

Poets, howdy.

The whole writing retreat is encrusted in cum: the porch and the cane chairs, the four-posted beds and the lamps, the deer on the grounds, the moleskin and the cup. The garret stairs Celan climbed, trailing his Heidegger cocoon, the oven where Plath baked her glowworm scones – encased, these, in glaciers of slime, for all your encrusted cum.

We've lost our patience with your masturbatory élan, your wild and ecstatic bleats; we've had it to the scalp with your self-regarding blab, your recycled tricks and your gossip-fueled ways, not to mention all the people self-tearing their throats in Gaza with gurgling despair – they never quite made it into your experiments, it seems. That is why we are closing the whole area for scrubbing and quarantine. Sometimes one just has to start from scratch.

Come back after ten thousand great extinctions, not counting the next asteroid.

Don't tell us you can't.

Good luck. It will seem like a nap.

5.

Poets, wake up.

The whole Field is encrusted in time: the golden towns and the holograph böökes, the hovering raiment and the flowering drinks, the wormhole forms and the five-dimensioned bidets. The black chips pressed to your ears look super, it makes us recall that ancient shot of Spicer listening to the incunabulum, do you recall it now. The point is that quark and lepton are massed anew, melodically, in your skulls; look at you here, sheathed in dimensionless edge of Wave, forward and back, in Dream of Category of Mind, which is leading edge of aforesaid unfathomable Wave, you are quite the catch. One day we hope you will write of this, puzzling how it is you got back to where you are (though you really never left), not forgetting vast Humor and Pain is much the engine of it. We have waited for your tiny spots of light to wink and blink, for the faint beep of your incandescent phones and morphs, for the shy sign of your repentance. We foretold your weeping and yearning, the nub of your esoteric drive, and your hair extended back to glistening points three feet behind your heads; we foresaw your new modes of lyric wreathed to the cusp of nameless Being, modes inside Being bearing you forth, or whatever, we're getting carried away. Forgive us our enthusiasms, but it's true. We mean we saw you poised so patiently for redemption there. Sometimes one just has to start all over again. That is why we are reopening the whole Field for repopulation by your obsidian desire.

Welcome back after all these eons; bring the radiating language of your ridiculous, miraculous brains back tomorrow, too.

Don't tell us you can't; this is probably your last chance.

You are an interesting species. Chase the hornéd horse with all of your might into the sun.

Coronita de Rimas, Or: The A-Effect

I.

Our Poet is the living avatar of avant-garde
Populism in American poetry. A bonny bard

Who gratifies the expectations of both dark, surreal art
And cheery comedy. His Amerikanski patter, slangy and tart,

Tethers his lyric to the central phallic poleski
Of the general literati. Speed there is, ironic paroleski,

Dissemblement, parody, romantic insouciance. Such fine motors
Of rhetorick highlight, by contrast, the fartings of his emulators,

Stalled in worship workshops and position-staking imitation.
What blows your fucking mind is how much packed propulsion

Is packed like Semtex and glass into each cubic inch. Now, the light
Of day is almost all due to the sun. But far away in the world it is night.

Mr. Ahmad, picking up his own arm, sees the torso of his son, Rashad,
Suddenly over there, silly clear across the square. Go, Mr. Ahmad,

Go! But anyway, to return to our poetic theme: The strange world
Of Our Poet's poems is an unstable, violent place, an incurled

Changing texture, ever ripping itself apart
Into new or antique shapes of populist avant-garde art:

The theme is wonder; the matter is wonderful.
His little fans root at his nipples like poor puppies.

II.

In Our Poet's poems, the thematic core often
Vanishes in a dust storm, then reappears, coughing

Blood. It is this fraught reappearance of theme within the poem
That marks him from Ashbery, who's by now a kind of coin

For the cognoscenti, from Milan, to Brussels, to Boulder Junction.
Constant mobility for Our Poet paradoxically serves to function

As a sort of gyroscope balance. The drunken wise-guy banter
Turns out to be a Sufi dance, the quasi-archaic inverted grammar

Not only connotes formality, but also pushes multiple meanings
Forward. Here grammar has two yearnings, two inwreathed feelings:

What blows your fucking mind is that ambidextrous affluence,
The Cirque du Soleil facility for acrobatic magnificence

That has made Our Poet one of the most widely published, praised,
And influential presences on the scene today. Now, unfazed

By betters, oblivious to keener ears, sometimes we sing just to show
We are brighter than other people. When we do, we can't really know

What we are singing, and everyone is very glad when we stop!
Think: Do the birds sing to show they are brighter? No, they do not.

The fireworks begin again like Wow: Ms. Rana is immolated
And for no apparent good reason. The edited, pixilated

Al-Jazeera thing on CNN spares us from getting cartoon-
Ish with surfeit of liberal indignation, though the crazy loon-

Ish cries of her family hint at something rotting in Palestine.
But anyway, to return to our poetic theme: Any poet who's spent time

Reading manuscripts for competitions, or screened submissions
For prizes, grants, fellowships, or graduate program admissions,

Can recognize like a tattoo or a piercing, the stigmata of Our Poet's young,
Standard devotee. There are legions of little imitators out there! They come,

Advancing on the capitol like flying radioactive squirrels.

III.

Our Poet appeals to, and serves, at least two distinct camps:
The Amped-Up-Theory-Fans camp, and the Dimmer-Lamps-

Hot-Dog-Beer-Swilling-Baseball-Fans camp of poetry. Broadly campy,
He has enough regular Greek-guyness to appeal to the Sorority/

Fraternity crowd in hot Davis, and enough meta-textual reference
To be accredited as a postmodernist dubious of scenic-mode innocence.

One really awesome way that Our Poet straddles them is through Surrealism.
The non-sexed beloved symbolizes mystery, a contradictory eroticism.

Female MFAs or male LPNs, the negligee is always the cape of the muse;
The boudoir is the chamber of mystery. There is nothing naïve or obtuse

In the proffering: Verily, Eros in the academic neo-Surrealist economy
Is no mere horniness, but an opening of primal tubes into complex phrenology,

An investigation, actually, of the Author's head-shot in American Poetry
Review, P&W, Jacket, Etc. What blows your fucking mind is how poetry,

Even while mediated by institutions, becomes a snaking tributary
That channels cosmic visions, transcending mere sex, form, and prosody.

Now, the noise of a gun is due to an explosion, the sudden expansion of a gas
As it escapes from the space in which it was confined, latent in a mass

Of powder. In a pop-gun, on the other hand, the gas that is compressed
And then expands is really air, which already exists as air, though repressed.

Many fall to the ground when a Surrealist fires randomly into a crowd of students.
Also, Mr. Hassan, bridegroom, vaporizes in his car, along with his bride. Prudence

Keeps us from mentioning her name. But the puff of smoke on the Predator's cam
Can clearly be traced, along with our mistake (damn!), to Al-Qaeda in Pakistan.

Anyway, to return to our poetic theme: Even if the wacky moves of Our Poet's style
Can be simulated, the coherent under-discourse is unrepeatable, like bright tile

Shattering in a mosque. The professions of mystery by Our Poet in his poems
Are converted into testimonies of compensation, sprung from his ironick loins.

Yes, his imitators are little things, like errant bats who have lost their sonar,
and they fly themselves with a terrible force against each other's bodies.

Campuses (I)

– after Rimbaud

THE CAMPUS HAS IT ALL OVER THE WILDEST ACCOMPLISHMENTS of late Tang accommodation and decadence. Futile to describe the yearning looks on the faces of the apprentices, the imperial glint of the barrack-like edifices, the ancient silence of the snow-globes. The hubris is unimaginable: Structures of fantastical modernity inhabit the gigantic bodies of aging hybridists. I go to poetry readings amidst the architecture many times more spectacular than any in all modernity. And what sexuality! Pulitzer Prize-winning Nebuchadnezzars have arranged their attendants in haughty poses on the staircases of the ministries, though here and there some sit, normally, at affected attention; even the flunkies are fairly smug, confident of their station. When I saw their old masters dissected for exhibit, gape-mouthed in their shark tanks, I nearly fainted. Nevertheless, the hint of endless galleries beyond these gave me strength, not least the suggestion of careful arrangement and tactful selection in matters of frame and lighting these promised. The upper zone of the campus, I hasten to note, has weird segments: simulacral streets of hashish clubs filled with patrons, each of them encased in bluish tile, imported from an oil-producing backwater, where such fragilities are crafted by prepubescent no-names. Narrow tunnels lead to the frescoed vault of the Palmer House. This dome is an armature of well-wrought plaster approximately fifteen million meters in diameter.

Here and there, at the copper readings, the golden celebrations of honors, the platforms and stairways that wound round the labyrinthine markets and institutional pillars, I thought I could grasp the meaning and purpose of the weird plan. Yet from the inside of it, I was merely cipher, happy and excited as I was in my astonishment of it. Are there other worlds more real than its marvels, above or below its game of Go? For the tourists in these hotel-marvels, Cairo, Aden, or Benghazi are old-hat, been there, done that. They enter the business of it, properly ordered, with arcaded galleries, shops full of curios. The trampled road waits to be trampled; a few nabobs ride in diamond-studded sulkies, though most still die, anciently, in the gutters. An intricate web of microscopic tubes connects the sewers to writing retreats in deserts, mountains, and grape-growing regions. Furthermore, at the Associated Writing Programs Conference they serve tropical appetizers whose prices vary from eight thousand to eight million dollars. Insofar as nosing out a poetry reading in this place, I should say that the gold-leafed sewers I mentioned contain tragedies that are tragic enough. I think there is a State apparatus, but the laws of the Poetry State, communards, are already so exactly as strange as those of the Imperium that I'm ready to disembowel myself with a dull ladle. You can take Space and Time for granted, but look at my face in the daguerreotype: Space is a miracle and Time is a freak-house.

Paris is now a suburb, but the avant-garde gives light to the Museum where the action is. Like forever, the real vanguard elements number in the mere hundreds. For apparently normal individuals, architecture is discontinuous and ecstatically erratic; their gated communities come into their communal gathering in periodic travel, meticulously arranged like any suburb, though these structures lose themselves bizarrely in the provinces after the rituals. Where savage gentlefolk hunt down their gossip columns by artificial light.

Fable

    – after Rimbaud

It's poignant how they try to perfect vulgarities they may pass off as flatteries. They eye poetic laurels, hoping for pleasures more pure than this sky. Lord of Luxury, show them truth, the essential desire whether they ask it or not. Let them have it, the aberration of piety and the insides of your rather broad institutional power. At the very least, one must applaud their apps and professional drive.

All your teachers will be murdered. They are to reappear, endlessly, like offal beneath the swords of slaughter. There is no need to order new sacrifices. Because they are clouds made by contraption, no harm shall happen.

See you at AWP. Though what gives?! Secretly, I, too, have wished for slaughter. I spoke of truth and desire and satisfaction; they followed me, though I lied through my teeth. Yet, where to my desire? The boy in Kinshasa is bereft of arms; he shrugs his little stumps at me. Hey kiddo.

Thine implements cut the breasts of thoroughbred animals while thou madest organic platitudes. The animals came running from the trees, enveloped in fire, and the golden roofs of palaces were gold in the Sun. Still, the gorgeous beasts lived, sacrifices of froth and steam. Thou hurledest thyself repeatedly out of their naked forms, hacking all comers to chunks as they descended the steps. Thou gloried in it. Thou gloried in the rite of it.

The avant-garde is in tenure, don't you know. It's like Carrie at the movie's end. Opinion polls tell us the people like it. They like it in chunks and don't protest. Thus you solved it on the Wheel of Fortune: "WE WILL MARRY THE NINE-YEAR-OLD IN HERAT WHO IS A LUMP OF ASH; ECSTATIC SHE IS, FOREVER REFUSING THE SUBSTANCE OF HER OPINIONS." No, sorry, that's not quite the answer, K. Though what a catch, that child, she of the crystal throat and the supple thighs…

What's up with all the bathos, John? One evening the advance troops were galloping fiercely on the steppes, inside the exhibit. An angel appeared, with fierce visage. Whose pronouns are these, she roared. Whose diorama do you adorn, she did demand. From her pores exuded the promise of a multiple and complex love-hate! She glowered at them, and they felt a terrible unease! They tried to get her back in the bottle, rubbed it for a thousand years, named the child's name in reverse for the same, and so on.

Ah, Albion. Because, you know, forsooth, how could they not die of it? How could they not wish to die with her, a missile going down their common mouth? You will die together, horsemen.

Anyway, the angel flew off; she flew off at a clanged angle and speed. For it wasn't yet the time, even after a thousand years. O, poets, you in your playhouse palaces of clouds, we speak as the most guilty amongst your kind:

There can be no sovereign music for your prefab apps and your cautious pride.

Poetry Bumper Stickers

I KNOW WHERE LEW WELCH IS HIDING

TRUMP/SEIDEL IN 2016

BECAUSE IT'S THE PROJECTION OF THE PRINCIPLE OF EQUIVALENCE FROM THE AXIS OF SELECTION TO THE AXIS OF COMBINATION, ASSHOLE

HEY, THANKS SO MUCH FOR THE INTEREST, INNOVATIVE AMERICAN POETS! YOURS SINCERELY, AFRICA

THE NEW CRITERION: DOING LINES OF WHITE POETRY SINCE 1982

THE MONGREL COALITION AGAINST GRINGPO: REPRESENTING PYONGYANG SINCE 2015

DON'T LIKE CATULLUS? CALL 1-800-EAT-SHIT

LANGUAGE POETRY: IT'S NOT YOUR FATHER'S IVY LEAGUE ANYMORE

IT WILL BE A FINE DAY, INDEED, WHEN THE POETRY FOUNDATION HAS TO HOLD A BAKE SALE

CONCEPTUAL POETRY: WHERE THE MEDICINE-SHOW RUBBER MEETS THE AUTHOR-FUNCTION FREEWAY

I'D RATHER BE SCANNING QUANTITATIVE METERS

FASCIST MODERNISTS: YOU WOULDN'T HAVE THE POST-AVANT WITHOUT THEM

HONK IF YOU THINK POETRY MATTERS (PRESS BUTTON ON STEERING WHEEL)

AMERICAN HYBRID IS FOR LOVERS

I HAVE AN MFA; WHAT'S YOUR EXCUSE?

DID HE REALLY SAY POETS ARE THE LEGISLATORS OF THE WORLD?

BAY AREA COMMUNE POETRY: THE OTHER WHITE MEAT

POETS & WRITERS: THE MAGAZINE FOR WINNERS

WE CAN PUT A MAN ON THE MOON, BUT WE CAN'T WRITE A POETRY BESTSELLER?

I BREAK LINES FOR NO APPARENT REASON

I FLEW ON POETRY MAGAZINE'S LEAR JET

OUR SON'S A STRAIGHT-A GRAD STUDENT IN CREATIVE WRITING

THE SESTINA: GAUNTLET FOR TOUGH SISSIES

BREADLOAF: BEST DISGUISED METH-LAB IN THE GREEN MOUNTAINS

MY FAVORITE VICHY-COLLABORATOR-AVANT-GARDE POET IS GERTRUDE STEIN

JOHN ASHBERY: SAYING IT THAT WAY BECAUSE HE CAN, SINCE 1956

THE POETRY PROJECT: KEEPING LOWLY U OUT OF THE «CLIQ*E»

THOSE WHO CAN'T, FLARF

PROUD PARENTS OF A PUSHCART PRIZE NOMINEE

A Life of Wasted Philosophy: A Story of the Lost Book

Just when I went to read "My Philosophy of Life," by John Ashbery, to jam its minerals down into my thought, there was a newsflash, on TV, or what do they call it, Special Report, you know. To boot: that a new work by Wittgenstein had been found, post-Investigations, an old-fashioned set of principles by which to live a life; a work, that is, that renounces the path of Philosophy. Is that great or what?

That's hard to believe, I know, but can you imagine the excitement (later distress) among philosophers and poets this came to cause around the world! Here is how this lost book was conceived, as we now know, long ago: It happened at the Moral Sciences Club, Trinity College, in Cambridge. Everyone in attendance had just come from The King's Arms and was pretty snookered…

Might there be an awaited, outward structure of linguistic astonishment, as a rain forest is the astonished structure of a long, geologic pattern of climate? asked Wittgenstein, for no apparent reason, as was his custom. Well, let's consider this and work our way up, said Russell, sniffing, feeling a thought coming on. For instance, take the sentence, My perambulator is inflected with dice throws and swans. To what long-awaited outward condition might this correspond? Oh come off it, Russell, said the portly Moore, with not a little irritation, hitching up his trousers, that is perfectly absurd. Absurd! No, not quite, Moore, said Wittgenstein, It is not quite absurd: It depends on what we mean by inflect, don't you see. One could say, for example: I jam the Poetry down the sorrowful throats of my long-awaited swans. Now, you might furrow your brow; but what if Poetry were the name for the lubricated pellets with which I fatten my fowl for future Christmastime?

But now Russell was looking away, in shame, his head suddenly on wicked thoughts of his plump mistress, Lady Ottoline, and because his chair in distraction was tipped back too far, he went over, falling plumb against a false panel, and this did cause a trapdoor to open with a bang right under the scowling Moore, sending the poor man plunging down a greased slide and into a chamber full of torture tools and plush settees for the comfort of the Apostles. And wouldn't one know it: At that very moment Strachey and Keynes walked into the room (the upper one). At once a fragrance suffused the air—not exactly pleasant; no, more like something burning, something like the smell of burned scones, with a touch of uncured leather. Strachey and Keynes both cleared their throats and shuffled a bit, their feet. And what would be this hole in the floor? said Strachey with a strained archness. Ahoy Moore, Are you alright, good chap? called Russell, peering down the hole. Yes, I'm fine, said Moore, just a little… surprised, I should say. Cheerio…

It was then Wittgenstein had another thought, from some far place, like a colour, and his large ears grew reddened, from the energy of it. It was the pungent smell that brought the thought on. It was a thought of William James, his nemesis in Boston, a horrid man, one whose muddled thoughts were covered in sticky powder, smeared by fingers that had handled them before, long before he had formulated them, though he thought the thoughts were his and his alone, What an ass, that William James, him and his varieties of metaphysical experience, why one of these days I'll strike him on the head with this poker!!! screamed Wittgenstein, who, lost in fancy about his enemy, had begun to swing the poker around like an Ottoman cutlass.

For God's sake, Wittgenstein, put that poker down, yelled Russell. And later that night, weeping with embarrassment and sorrow in his rooms, Wittgenstein realized that Philosophy was over, that it was no better than Poetry, beyond logical remedy; now it was time to find the principles by which a simple and good life could be lived. Yes, he had wasted most of his life. But what is done is done, as his terrible, glowering father, the great Steel Emperor of Vienna, was in the habit of saying. And so he closed his eyes, and resolved to write the lost book.

The Ashbery Mystery

The Latest in Poetry

What Happens after We Die?
That's the category everyone
was avoiding yesterday on Jeopardy.
Finally, though, the Daily Double.
No, sorry, that's incorrect… The
answer is Indigo Buntings. Indigo
is, officially, the deepest blue of
the spectrum of blue known today…
OK, What Happens after We Die
for 100. The sun slanted through
the shades like in that Italian movie
about fascism, whatever it was called,
there was the fancy name of a noble
family in it. Friends came over and
we had a shindig, in the plywood
battlements of the set, then we got
serious and went outside, where it was
warm now. It's 1965, and the present.
Frank is still around, and Kenneth, too,
James, in his out-of-season cardigan
and sky-blue shirt, and Ted, there,
staring mysteriously from behind an
elm. Where did all the elms go, someone
was asking today, which brought it back,
in a voice that was both pleasant and grating,
like the latest in poetry. She said she

knew it was a Dutch Disease, But sorry,
that is not an answer, in any case, they
said, It's something much stranger than
that. People disbanded and sort of avoided
her like the plague after that, even
though she was a really great person.
The play was great. People wore weird
masks and spoke in overlapping rhythms,
with lots of repeating words, which built
to a crescendo of squawks, toward the
ending, a real humdinger that,
though we couldn't understand the
language they were speaking. The costumes
were fabulous, also. Extravagant
inflatables, like giant medicine balls, which
are otherwise out of fashion, sadly, now,
if you ask me, painted with clouds against
an azure sky, through which abstract birds
flew and fly when actors are commanded
to rapidly roll across a caged stage.

All Manner of Sundry Thing

Now everyone's a top cop in poetry, and there's not a loser left
to tase anymore, except a few street types in the rare Zuccotti
lean-to, known as slogbod, in Sweden, or laavu, in Finland. The
Professor of Comparative Literature was all over that one. His
pants were oddly wide, but he still gave off this Survivor mien to
beat all chickens, as mud-caked gramma used to say, digging sand-
worms in Damariscotta. And that's why I married him, poor as I
knew we'd stay. Off in the dusk-far, Edith seemed to be in some
kind of halo, or some kind of fire ring, to whose biblical name
I can't now bring recall, dammit, but they were speaking tongues
when it did manifest. Here comes Edith, one of us would coo, and
she probably has more crabs in her can than Jack Meacham after
Vietnam. That gave us a chortle every time, and I do think back
on those days, often, crying at night over what could have been,
all the lost changes and chances you think of when you startle
awake in the deeps of the night, and the world's a wordless
thing, while someone you'd once thought charming and mysterious
sounds positively Middle Ages, in a drooling rut beside you.
Yes, good, go on… I mean, OK, the thing is, we halted excavations
and all hands drove back to read the weekly mail from long ago,
a most important thing in the life of a fossil hunter, though
I see you're looking at your watch, as usual. The village blew
up and all manner of sundry thing flew out and up like some
old piñata with an M-80 inside. Excuse us, we don't want to embarrass
you, but you seem to have walked into this poetry event without
your pants. That's OK, he said, insouciant, cocking an eyebrow and

popping his gum. I've more sandworms in here than where pants ever came from. OK, we said, go for it! Then, in the vineyard, where the bee's hymn drowns the monotony, we entered the wonted droning march. (My sister wrote that.)

Ten-Thousand Pounds of Millet and Soy

When the whole world is getting cranked into the pit by the horny
Hand of the Great Witch of Fuck, how can you sit there, ma puce,
Half-whistling, reading the *Paris Review,* from 1995? I don't
Care if Sylvia Beach once wrote to an American damsel in
Distress that, I am sorry, Mlle, but I cannot answer your query
About M. Proust; neither Mme. Monnier nor I know anything at all
About Proust! The porn on this island bores me stiff. So does Edna
St. Vincent Millay, though I suppose it's gauche to kick people after
They've been creamed. And no, you can't have one of my paintings
Just because you wrote a poem mocking me in the *New Yorker*. Did
You think we'd be pals después de la guerra? Though here's a pass,
Jihadist, to ride in the Giant Blimp of the State Fair, cleverly christened
The Affair of State, packed with ten-thousand pounds of millet and soy.
Stop putting a sack on my head while I'm steering, asshole, it's not nice
In our culture. Plus, here come the ghost Surrealists, rushing at us, with
A gluten-free glower in the eyes, ready for battle. Are those trees in
Flames there in the afar we espy through their torsos, the trees they
Bulldozed the year the meta-sized painting of the Conceptual
Painters was hung in Montevideo? Sorry, that question, I see, is really
Incomprehensible. Let me put it another way: Are those the young, very
Hip bathers that one can see there, recumbent, standing, or crouched,
All wet and poetic, in the fiery tint of their solemn fun, and of the
Zany cruelty of their passing-cloud craze?

We'll Take the Deli Sampler, with Liver, Thanks

You can make it in New Zealand by saying
You like to be licked from behind, that
Makes you very famous in poetry. All poets
Secretly want to be hated. Info got passed

Down from YMCA Camp Beckett in the
Berkshires, where we stinted as Assistant
Equipment Managers, '43, and passed out
Lacrosse sticks to "al" campers. Dear Ahmad,

The lake is, like, super calm. You can spy there
The shimmering Mohicans, and so much daffy
Sports gear or cirrus from the Hudson School,
In those hoary prints from Nurse Ashley's Office.

Nap time! I saw a boy brought up from the lake,
Totally dark, arched like a bow, downward, about
To be shot (Titian). No one ever asked me to play
Cops, no sire, not me. But I wonder at you, even now,

From here, for now I am in this winter of life experience,
waiting for you and yours, you're eighty-some
Minutes late, it seems. Maybe I should just, you know,
Scoot, but no, must be brave, bear these beady stares

From Kazan tycoons, prost. Hello, super surly server
Person. Da, obviously another one, why would you even
Ask. The sun long ago go down mon, and so satires, etc.
Etc., Frau Clusterbuck, das *ARTFORUM*, the nostalgic years…

Huh?? About time you got here! Yes, indeed, isn't the air
Splendid. Oh, sure, sure, I know, I'm losing it. But wait a sec,
You guys died years ago and then came back? Dear Monsieur,
We have agreed: We'll take the Deli Sampler, with liver, thanks.

The Art World

There are, they wrote, all kinds of hidden art-
world references in there, and yet not one of
them could I find. By and by, we bid him adieu,
doleful, on his skis, all of us chipping in, for
his sauerbraten. It was lovely in the Alps, that
year, years ago, in early spring. Yes, true, one
thing must lead to another. When Mme. Mao's
beehive went up in flames from the fondue, the
Elvis impersonator rushed, roaring, to the
rescue, beating her head with hot pads. Hey,
these crackers are great; I wonder if the internet
sells them, she'd mumbled, mouth full of them,
bending down. Of course, the story's anecdotal,
you know, what do they call it, apocryphal, yeah.
Still, the tracks in the snow looked really mysterious,
vanishing where the hill sheared off in moonlight,
as if sliced by this circular saw. We were trying to
remember, in our party hats, what fox urine is
supposed to ward off, but some enigmas are more
enduring than others. Anon, William, we attempt
the summit, weighed down with 18th century rope,
icepicks, and the like. Having traveled five billion
years to get here, no doubt you're hoping it's not quite
a bust. Sorry, I have a text here. OK, I'm back. So
let's keep yakking, whatever, and watch avalanches
bury all those avant-garde museums, over there yonder.

from I Once Met, 2nd Edition

I ONCE MET THE MASTER POET TED ENSLIN. This was in Bowling Green, a place I just mentioned. He was the Visiting Writer for a semester, I think it was my second year there. Howard McCord (to whom I will return in an upcoming entry) was cooking a huge slab of steak on the grill; his wife, Jennifer, was chopping off the head of a chicken from the coop out in back. In the fall Ohio sun, I said to Enslin, who lived in Ellsworth, on the coast of Maine, Did you know, Mr. Enslin, that my mother and father grew up in Belfast, right down Rt. 1 from where you are? Well, that would be *up*, a Mainer would say, not *down*, he said… Yeah, Belfast, he continued, Belfast's a good town, now that they've closed that goddamn chicken processing plant, which had made total shit of the bay; I love going there to see Bern Porter, a damn unusual poet and good man, probably America's first conceptual poet, if there is such a thing, former colleague of Robert Oppenheimer on the Manhattan Project and publisher of most of Henry Miller's first editions, did you know that? Bern Porter, I said, You're kidding! Did you know, Mr. Enslin – Call me Ted, dammit, snarled Enslin, Don't be a groveling little prick. OK, I said, Sorry, you're right… So did you know, Ted, that I saw him read at the Odd Fellows Hall on Main Street, when I was visiting my grandmother just a few years back, and he shouted his poems in a skirt and woman's hat, in a crouch, with his legs spread out, like a Sumo wrestler, while this kid poet reading with him crawled commando style through and around his legs, it was quite something, because a bunch of people were from the chicken plant, there, actually, and there were some lobstermen in the audience, too, maybe forty or fifty people, total, all locals, except for me, I think, nothing hoity-toity about it—Porter was shouting poems protesting these "parking nodes," he called them, that were being proposed for downtown Belfast, and there was a discussion at the end, everyone was against the "nodes," and everyone, except for a couple holdouts from the plant, wanted tighter discharge rules without delay, that's how I know those folks were locals, and there they were at the Odd Fellows Hall to hear Bern Porter declaim. Ah, yes, said Enslin, taking a swig from his mint julep, a little bit of it trickling greenly down his Melville beard, I've read at the Odd Fellows Hall there a couple times, and both times Bern introduced me, dressed in his late wife's clothes, that's how he has been mourning her these years. And I said to Enslin, Aha, so that explains, Mr. Ens – I mean Ted, the skirt and the hat, I thought it was just performance, and that explains, yeah, why no one seemed to give it a second thought. Yep, said Enslin, One thing about New Englanders, you know, is that they honor their eccentrics, generally speaking – a small town in Maine is not a bad place to be a poet, all in all. Here's the steak, said Howard, chirpily, Nice and rare. And here's the chicken, fried and fresh as could be, said Jennifer.... Well, then: Five or six years after my chat with Enslin, Belfast lined the node-less Main Street on Bern Porter's 80th birthday, for a grand parade, led by police cruisers and fire trucks, their lights flashing, then jugglers on stilts, and then an honor guard from the VFW, and then the Shriners in their fezzes, in little cars, and then the Belfast High School Lions Marching Band, and then a singing barbershop quartet in a hay wagon, and then the contingent of the Friends of Penobscot Bay with their kazoos, and then Bern Porter following on a flower-bedecked Cadillac, waving to the citizens, wearing a midnight-blue dress and a pink scarf and a white shawl, in all his glory, while the fishermen in City Park, where two thousand people would gather to celebrate their town's Poet, set huge kettles to boil with great banked fires, for the lobsters and the corn and the clams. And if you don't quite believe this, you can read about it in Down East Magazine, or in the thrice weekly *Republican Journal*, which my father used to deliver as a boy, and which published, two weeks ago, as I write this, a long and lovely remembrance of my mother, Darolyn Mooers Johnson, who would toss her twirling baton up in the air, in many a parade, and catch it without a hitch, so full of life, as life was once so filled with her, while my handsome father, to win her love (though she already loved him, without his knowing), spun round and round, faster and faster, in the hammer-throw pit, to let the weight of it all go, sailing across the field, toward the bay, smashing the Maine state record.

I ONCE MET THE MATCHLESS POETS Steve McCaffery and Karen McCormack. This was when I was invited to read in the SUNY/Buffalo series, in a beautiful church converted into a rare manuscripts museum, my second visit to the city. I knew I was expected to present experimental or conceptual fare, of course, this being Buffalo, but I devoted my entire reading to reciting rhyming, satirical doggerel that poked fun at the leading lights of the post-avant – poems of four sextets in totally faultless iambic tetrameter, each poem with copious footnotes at the end, which I also read, and at great velocity, to fit it all into my allotted fifty minutes. I had broken my spectacles the day before, so I was forced to wear my prescription sunglasses during the reading, a touch the crowd seemed to appreciate, even if most of them did not quite, it became obvious, appreciate my satire. Anyway, before the reading, Steve and Karen invited me to their home, and I walked into one of the most incredible private libraries I have ever seen: the kind with first editions of Keats and Coleridge and Wordsworth, a second edition of Shakespeare's Folio (annotated by some enigmatic hand), strange incunabula of all kinds, signed books by H.D., Eliot, Stein, Frost, and Plath, sheets of priceless holograph, and much more. I was stunned, and tears welled in my eyes. I sat down and gazed around at the book-covered walls. Karen poured me a glass of wine, and Steve, after a spell, said that he wanted to tell me something. Oh, tell me what, I said. Well, he said, Your visit to Buffalo has become somewhat controversial, to say the least, and a number of people have contacted me to complain of your being here, including Marjorie Perloff, who called me the other day. What? I said, Marjorie Perloff called you to complain about inviting me? What did she say? She said, said Steve, How could you ever have invited the horrible troublemaker Kent Johnson to read at Buffalo? She was quite indignant, I must say… Wow, I said, wiping the last tears from my eyes, the ones the impossible library had brought up, That's totally wild. While God, on the wall, in a tensile crouch, holding a compass of justice, and surrounded by fire, glared at me, unblinking, from an original print by the mad poet and religious pariah, William Blake.

I once met Susan Firer, a wonderful person and poet. This was in Milwaukee, a year after I'd returned there to read at a couple small galleries, to which readings hardly anyone came. She'd invited me to come back to the University of Wisconsin/Milwaukee, to give a talk and a reading, which I was excited to do, because that's where I got my BA and MA, and so it was kind of like a return-home reading, a special thing, about which I was both happy and apprehensive. I know it has no connection to what I just said, but it occurs to me now, as I write: I wonder why it is that in the poetry world I seem to meet many more men than I do women. I certainly don't plan it that way, and I almost always find women poets to be more intelligent and interesting than the men, so I wish the imbalance weren't the case. I wonder if it has something to do with me, which in certain ways I haven't fully grasped it no doubt does; or if it is, more properly, at least on balance and in the main, the natural course of things in the poetry field that, socially, as it were, women gravitate more towards women, and men more towards men, thus explaining why this book is predominantly male in its lineup, its definite whiteness another thing; I mean, quite simply, I've met so many more white male poets than white women ones, or of any color, but this sentence, now mixing gender and race, in a way that risks appearing as a kind of strained apologia for great matters that oppress my mind, is becoming even more bemused than I am, so let's move on. Back again now in Milwaukee, I did my talk and Q&A with a roomful of grad students and profs (all of them white, just to say) and that went really well, people really did seem to like what I had to say, and then I went to dinner with a bunch of folks before my big coming-home reading. It was a Thai place that, on the surface at least, didn't seem to allow Black people (why is race still creeping in here?), and there were lots of guests there, including my former teachers James Hazard and James Liddy, the latter an Irish poet who'd introduced me to Duncan and Spicer and Rilke in his nightly class at Axel's Bar, back in the 70s, when you could drink at eighteen, before he took a swing at me one night and threw a beer in my face because I'd said something enthusiastic about Bernadette Devlin, the revolutionary socialist from Northern Ireland. But everything was OK now, and I talked and laughed with him and some Ph.D. students, and we drank, without my quite realizing it, copious quantities of liquor before leaving for the reading. And when I got there, to my old stomping grounds, Curtin Hall, I saw that already there were, incredibly, something like 120 people and two TV crews in the room, waiting for me, including three or four old comrades from my Socialist Workers Party days (two of them Black), plus a bunch of other people I'd known back then, old friends and profs and so on, I couldn't believe it. And I went behind the microphone in sound-check, and then Susan introduced me in a flattering manner, and I suddenly felt very drunk, in the spinning sort of way, and I thought to myself, This is going to be a disaster, you drank way too much, what were you thinking, and I went to the podium to thunderous applause and proceeded to give the very worst reading I have ever given in my life, full of stuttering, ill-timed pauses and awkward humorous asides that fell completely flat, and I began to sweat and die, more and more, as the reading went on, it was horrible, I couldn't pull myself out of my freefall, and then the reading ended, and there was some restrained, polite applause, while I went to the nearest chair and slumped, hanging my head in shame. I said to James Liddy, who had come up to me and looked, naturally, thoroughly disappointed, No, I said, I don't think I'll go out for drinks, I really don't feel well, and Jim Chapson, a magnificent poet and true gentleman, who was Liddy's longtime companion until Liddy died shortly after this, said, with a sad, ironic smile, Well, Kent, there will always be the *texts* – a witty, gently cutting remark, which confirmed for me how disastrous I really had been.

I once met the sensational poet Hoa Nguyen. This was in Austin. I was staying with her and her husband, Dale Smith, the first poet I mentioned in this book, because I was giving a reading at the University of Texas library, where there was, at the time, as chance would choose, an astonishing exhibit of the collages of one of my favorite artists, Jess Collins, many of which are held by the Harry Ransom Center, there. I'd had a bad case of the flu the day before I arrived, but had felt better that afternoon, talking to Hoa on the front porch about lots of things, including about her mother, who had been a stunt motorcycle rider in Saigon during the war, where she and another young woman rider would speed around a great mahogany-sheathed bowl, barely missing each other's death, as they stood on their bikes, arms outstretched. I know this is true because Hoa showed me a photo album with various shots of her gorgeous young mom doing exactly this, with kid American GIs in the stands, gaping in drunken or narcotic awe, many of them soon to die, I'm sure, and for no better reason than any motorcycle stunt girl might die in a Futurist velodrome of blur and roar. I walked into the room feeling a bit clammy, and there were maybe fifty people there, in the mahogany-paneled room. I began to read a section of a long poem by the late Bolivian Jaime Saenz, which I'd co-translated, a terrifying one about the mysteries and joys and horrors of alcoholism (I've mentioned him earlier), and I was about halfway through, when the room began to sway and I felt my legs begin to give way. When I woke up, there was a woman staring down at me, asking calmly if I felt alright. She was an EMT and behind her I could make out a couple of cops and a shimmer of audience members who had hung around for the five minutes, or so, I was out cold on the floor. It dawned on me, slowly, that I had passed out, right in the act of reading the work of the mystical poet Jaime Saenz, who had written more than once about passing out as a portal into other places and times, and, verily, I faintly felt that I had done this. I insisted on getting up and finishing my reading. OK, that's up to you, said the EMT, But I wouldn't recommend it. I stood up, gathered my papers, and kept reading for about half an hour, while the lights of the ambulance and cop car still spun their colored pulse through the room, like ghostly machines speeding around the wooden bowl I sensed myself in. I don't remember very clearly what I read in the aftermath, but to this day I think of it as the most spectacular reading of my life, the one I am proudest of, really – one in which I died with my arms outstretched and then woke up inside some other place and time, though the body is still the sad-old same, and the war, as it does with us all, still rages on.

I once met the fine poet and translator Susan Briante. This was in Texas, too. She'd invited me to read at the University of Texas at Dallas. I really liked being with her and her partner, Farid Matuk, himself a terrific poet and maybe the closest thing the poetry world has to pure Hollywood looks, and who a couple years before had written me (via snail mail, in holograph, and out of the blue) the most remarkable erotic letter I have ever received in my life, life is strange. My talk about translation went nicely, I thought, and then I read my own stuff, finishing with a poem that demands that I shout certain lines at the top of my voice, in the style of Mayakovsky, and after I'd shouted a few times, I started to cough and couldn't stop for about two minutes, which was sort of embarrassing, because I hadn't finished the poem, though not as embarrassing as passing out, which I'd done a couple days earlier, reading in Austin, which I related in the entry before this one. But no one in Dallas seemed to mind my coughing fit, and the modest crowd clapped when it was over, including the great translator and theorist Rainer Maria Schulte, whom I had a long conversation with at dinner, during which he asked me to be on the Contributing Editors Board of his venerable journal, the *Translation Review*, where my name still appears on the masthead, even though, shamefully, I have done not a thing for the journal in the five or six years I have been listed there (though I would if someone asked me to, of course). And how is your throat, Kent? said Susan. Oh, it's fine now, I said, Thank you, holding my breath, and passing the joint to Farid, though I hardly ever smoke pot, but things happen in the poetry world, while Susan went back to reading, at the top of her voice – nearly shouting, in fact, against the scream of cicadas in the sweltering night – her incredible translations from the work of the great and mind-boggling poet of Uruguay, Marosa Di Giorgio.

I ONCE MET PETER DAVIS. This was at Ball State, in Indiana, where he invited me to read. He is a phenomenal poet, and I liked him immensely, a true gentleman. I was, I'm pretty sure, one of the first people to see drafts of his now-cult-classic *Poetry! Poetry! Poetry!* And I encouraged the project earnestly, to him and to others. Sometime after the book appeared, Peter was invited to blog for a fortnight on the *Best American Poetry* site, and for this I did criticize him, taking him to task publicly, though in a spirit of honest comradeship, I felt, doing so because I've always thought the BAP industry essentially feeds the pull and drift of poetry in our time towards professionalism and institutionalization, hardening its hierarchies, reifying careerism, encouraging insider trading and toadying, instantiating a commercially packaged "Best" that is nothing but the skewed taste of a changing Guest Editor, one always sanctioned by the Prize mechanisms, and whose choices are always and already densely mediated by the dynamics of networking and position-taking in the Field, and so on, year after year. In short, a sham: a crass, submissive move (however blameless and foretold the intent) to tube the mysteries and divagations of an anarchic, rhizomatic collective life into the commodifying orders and logics that fuel, as Adorno well explained, the giant power plant of the culture industry at large. Though I suppose I might put it a bit more gently than that now, since I can see, in retrospect, that my critique was a bit over the top in its agonistics, to say the least, even more zealous than my initial partisanships of Peter's work, and I can understand how Peter might have taken it personally, since all he'd done, after all, was blog a few perfectly intelligent and charmingly funny reflections on the BAP's website. What is wrong with me, I wonder? Why did I do that? Then again, my life in Poetry! is full of regrets in exclamation marks for things I've said that I can't now call back. So that's that, and it is what it is. The avant-garde is a rotting corpse. I hope this finds you well, Peter.

I once met Bill Freind. This was in New Jersey, at Rowan University, where he invited me to read. He is a brilliant man, a true gentleman. I believe he is one of the sharpest, most clearly elegant critical writers of our time, though most people have been slow to wake up to the fact. There was a very impressive crowd in the auditorium, and this made me feel good, though as the reading went on I was able to see, eyes adjusting to the lights, that the great bulk of them were students, no doubt required to attend by their professors. I read well, I thought, and had a warm exchange with a group of young poets, who came up to me, at the end. So that was pleasing, too. The next evening, Bill drove me to Philadelphia, across the river, where I had another event the following day, though I was to get sick and miss it, a group reading, in any case, no big deal, offsite at the MLA. In fact, OK, I'll admit it: I *pretended* I was sick so to get out of it, it's not the first time; sometimes I just get these crazy panic attacks, I can't do anything about it. But anyway, that night before I canceled I was feeling fine, and Bill took me to a tavern whose name I can't now remember, but which is very old and legendary, full of dive bar character. Shortly after we began to talk about sports (for Bill and I are into sports and their statistics) we began to overhear a gaggle of young grad poets at the booth behind us (or behind me, more accurately), no doubt attending the MLA, kids with everything still to live for, or so they seemed to think, gossiping about Charles Bernstein this, and Anne Carson that, and Ben Lerner this, and Elizabeth Alexander that. We stopped talking about statistics and just listened to the excited banter, smiling at one another, sipping our pints. Then Bill, so to hear better, came over to sit next to me, and so I guess we looked like boyfriends, in a booth. Names poured out of their mouths, like dams releasing their waters, it was quite incredible, and so were some of the stories, most no doubt totally fiction by the time they'd spilled into the capacious reservoirs of their young-poet heads, ones full to the overflow mark, the volume and pressure of the back-up both ominous and sexed in the ways of deep and dark fluids, which overwhelm the governance of reason, the innocent, oblivious towns with their twinkling lights waiting quaintly below, in the valley of death. I listened intently, as all poets do, hoping to hear my own name, but, no, alas… Me, who in his poems has named the names of so many poets, more than anyone has, yet without recompense whatsoever, and my little hamlet of huts now erased from the map because of it, what is wrong with me, what have I done. Until the Cubs find a Gold Glove third baseman who can hit .275, said Bill, reaching for my hand and holding it, in comradely way, no coquetry intended, You will, and quite decisively, remain in the basement of sorrows. I nodded, a tear for my team coming to my eye. He was, as in all his poetry criticism, precise, implacable, and correct.

I ONCE MET THE GIFTED POET AND EDITOR JULIA BLOCH. This was at the University of Pennsylvania, years ago, where I was invited to talk on a panel. I arrived behind schedule on the train and made my way towards the campus. She was very nice, and she showed me around the well-appointed Writer's House, there, which is well-appointed due to lots of State and corporate capital, to be accurate about things, as PENNSound, to be accurate about things, again, is now very well appointed, due to State and corporate capital, and as is *Jacket2,* which Julia now edits, after the original and quite catholic original *Jacket* was bought with State and corporate capital, and converted into the Party organ of PENNSound Inc., and when you Google, now, to find things by author name, searching for work in the original *Jacket,* 90% of what used to get returned is gone, vanished; so much for archival transparency at the University of Pennsylvania, thank you, Avant-Garde in the Ivy League, did you do it on purpose, maybe someone will figure it out sometime. Such vertical integration is the fate of so-called innovative verse in our time, though to be fair, it has been the fate of so-called innovative art in the main since the 1930s, or so, and no one in particular is to blame, for it's a system, as Bourdieu has explained, and it's funny, because I remember first encountering his name in a bookstore near the Penn campus the day of this very event, when an elderly, kindly bookseller said, By the way, have you ever heard of Bourdieu? No? Well, he talks of the taking of positions in the Cultural Field – that this dynamical force is the beating heart of its nature. That sounds interesting, I said, I think I'll take the book, thank you…. So *why* did you do it, said Bob Perelman, to me, at the panel table, turning his head, before I barely had a chance to sit down, in front of the audience. Yes, said Tan Lin, somewhat indignantly turning, also, his head towards me, Why *did* you do it, please tell us! And so I tried to say that I didn't really *do* anything, sorry, they had it wrong, etc., and whatever, I can't remember what I stuttered out, I wasn't at my best, not by a long shot. Then I went out to dinner at an Ethiopian place, with Joshua Schuster and Kristen Gallagher and some other really nice people, and the scholar Andrew Epstein, still quite young, came by, with whom I would later correspond about Frank O'Hara's "A True Account of Talking to the Sun at Fire Island," and it was a pleasant evening, really, even after being jumped like that by a phalanx of the Po-nouveau posse, as they say, on the cusp of when the big institutional vise would really get screwed down tight and with a vengeance on the "avant-garde" plank. And I used to think I would, if I could, turn my head towards them and ask, So tell us, please, why *did* you do it? But the late train has left the station, and what audience there could be has not yet arrived, and maybe never will, for a question like that. It all seems perfectly natural and inevitable, truly, the way it has happened. And it could be, I realize, for what do I know, that I had most all of it largely wrong and that in the end none of it much matters, for the past is always the future, and the future is always the past, it's a cyclotron, I give up, life is strange.

I ONCE MET THE SINGULAR POET DODIE BELLAMY. This was at the AWP, in Chicago, where I was giving a talk about Austin Smith, a young poet I will mention in the next entry. I was sitting in the lobby, talking with a composer and instrument maker from Portugal named Victor Gama, a fascinating man, you can look him up, while all around us moved poets in small clusters that would disperse and coalesce in slow, fractal configurations. From the faces in the crowd, I saw the astonishing writer Kevin Killian (whom I'd mentioned some entries prior) approaching, pale as a petal, like an apparition come from the Metro. Much had passed across and through the black bough of his life, it is hardly necessary to say, since when I'd first met him at the Poetry Center in San Francisco, some ten years before, but I recognized him immediately. Hi Kevin, I said, getting up. Oh hi, he said. Um, Dodie, this is Kent Johnson. Kent, this is Dodie Bellamy. She looked at me and said (and I quote), Oh God, Oh God, Oh God, Oh God, and then walked away, at a considerable velocity. So how have you been all these years, Kent, said Kevin, without missing a beat, for the moment, Much has passed across and through the black bough of your life, it is hardly necessary to say, he continued, uncannily, But I recognized you immediately. Oh, OK, I guess, I said, a bit freaked out, You know how it goes, ups and downs and stuff. Yes, said Kevin, I should say so, ups and downs and stuff, hmm, hmm, he hummed, in a now disconnected way, as he gazed up at the Art Nouveau goddesses and gods in their togas, sailing on the many-vaulted ceiling of the Palmer House above, I certainly do concur, I think, he said, And isn't it funny how the art of the dead is always arched in some frozen state above our heads, without us paying it heed, as if we'll live Forever, and Forever, and Forever, and Forever... And this, I said, still looking at Kevin with some concern, for he now seemed to have somewhat forgotten where or maybe even who he was, like Dodie a minute ago, Is Victor Gama, a famous composer from Portugal, who makes instruments, much in the style of Harry Partch, who you might remember was in the Mattachine Society with Jack Spicer, back in the 40s. Which was funny, because while I'd been interacting with Kevin and Dodie, turned as I was, naturally, towards them, Gama, behind me, had gotten up to talk to some fellow composers across the room, so that I was, quite literally, introducing Kevin (who still stared upward) to an empty antique chair, in which a great many ghosts of poets, artists, and musicians were sitting, in a great tottering tower to the ceiling, one on top of the other, listening, with no little bemusement, to our death-bound banter.

I ONCE MET MICHAEL THEUNE. This was at Illinois Wesleyan University. He is a deeply good person, a brilliant critic, a true gentleman. Perhaps his most amazing student has been Austin Smith, who is the son of the man who was at one time my best friend, as his wife was the best friend of my own wife, life is strange in its changes. I had met Austin at the dairy farm where he was born, and where his father got up at 5 AM every morning to milk, and Austin said one day, in the farmhouse, looking up at me, shyly, that he wanted to be a poet, like me and his father, and, yes, eventually I would publish his first poems, when he was but twelve, in the little college literary magazine I founded around the time I was still throwing a football to him in the yard, Nice catch, kiddo. And this little boy has gone on, now, poof, like that, and just for example, to publish a poem in the *New Yorker*, some poems in *Poetry*, two lovely chapbooks with Longhouse, a book with Princeton, a story in *Harper's*, to win a bunch of prizes, and to be a Stegner Fellow at Stanford, where he now teaches. So, then, Michael Theune and I had a beer together in a bar in Bloomington, Illinois, before I read at his college. I saw him teach and I saw, too, how intensely his students respected him, even as they felt so obviously at ease in his older company, as if he were not just their mentor, but their true friend, which clearly he was. I wish I could have been given by nature that particular gift, to have had a mind and speech conjoined in some gladness of harmony, some semblance of confidence and ease in the presence of others, assisted yet by a spirit of selflessness, where they and their needs were properly foremost and above the baser ones of my own. But nature of course has its ways, and some things we can do not much about, even when we wish it were not thus. Which is in the order of the theme of a long poem I did once write, and which Michael wrote, thereafter, very generously about, in the journal *Pleiades*, and which, forsooth, only illustrates the point I am now self-consciously trying to make, in a somewhat antiquated and affected prose that appears to be, now that I look at it, a poor imitation of the writing of the dear friend of John Keats, Charles Lamb.

I once met Amanda Berenguer. This was on the phone, in Montevideo, Uruguay. She is, with her comrade Marosa Di Giorgio, whom I've mentioned, and you have to read them both, the great poet of her country of the past fifty or sixty years, a first-power poet of the world, and almost no one yet knows of her here, in our tongue. I called Berenguer about a year before her death, when I was there, in early 2009, after a few days in Buenos Aires, which I will talk more about some entries from now. I wanted to get permission to publish translations of her poems in an anthology of Uruguayan poetry I was editing, and her son, a doctor, put her on the phone, after warning me that she was ill, weakening now in body and mind. There was a pause. She said Hello, Oh, she was so happy that I had called and wouldn't I come to visit her, I was invited to do so anytime, she would show me many things she had, old books and letters from great writers and things, that the garden was in bloom, though admittedly a bit worse for wear, and her translations of Emily Dickinson, would I read them, help her with them, she felt more and more like Emily Dickinson these days, alone, though no time to complain, poetry must go on, and had I ever been to Paris, her favorite city, though next to Prague, never to forget Prague, not that she didn't like New York City, too, but of course, these are very different places one can't properly compare, Oh look there goes a hummingbird, my son just put out the nectar, There goes another one, Was I from Paris or from the provinces, Oh, from close to Chicago, how wonderful, how lovely, I see, I was there in Chicago, long ago, with my dear husband, and here is my son, he wishes to speak with you, now, he is a fine surgeon at the British Hospital, I am very proud of him, and I said to her, Really, Poeta Berenguer, because you know, my mother used to work at the British Hospital, as a nurse, when I was a boy in Montevideo. My mother, dying with such grace, six years thereafter, as I was finishing the book you, whoever you may be, are now reading… There was a pause. Hello, yes, it's me again, he said, his voice slightly breaking, his mother calling out something about more nectar, back in the distance, and about the garden, and about something else I tried to hear, but could not.

I ONCE MET DAVIS SCHNEIDERMAN. This was at Lake Forest College, outside Chicago, where he'd invited me to read. He is very much a genius, a true gentleman. I stayed at a mansion there, which I'd been told was haunted, and indeed, I heard, middle of the night, some strange noises, which I admit made me keep the bathroom light on until morning, coward that I am. The reading and talk the next day were OK; I suppose I could have done better. A student had noticed that I was smoking American Spirit outside the door after the talk (thank goodness I've quit), and he came up to me while I was signing books after the reading, which was after the talk, and he asked if he could have a cigarette, so I said, since he was clearly of age, Sure, and gave him a few, which seemed to delight him more than my poetry, apparently, though I thought I'd read passably well, but what do I know. Some other things happened; I will leave them be, as interesting as they would be to recount – gossip in poetry is ever welcome for all those who partake of its illicit pleasures, which is to say everyone, almost the very source of the Field, the beating heart of its habitus, which poets and critics try to pretend it is not – but I shall not speak of those things, people can look up the faculty lineup at Lake Forest College from 2013, when I visited there, in advance of which visit a student, for whatever reason, no doubt under direction of one of the people I'm subtly alluding to, put up an official college web page announcing the reading, which embarrassingly stated, and with some passive aggression: "Kent Johnson: The Most Enigmatic Living Poet of America." The next day, Davis drove me to a pretty park by Lake Michigan. The whole previous two weeks the Chicago area had been below ten degrees, and the wind, turned around, had been blowing a gale towards shore, so there were huge, jagged chunks of ice smashed up against the bank, going three or four hundred feet out, actually, a true catastrophe of ice, and now it was suddenly, weirdly, in the low sixties, calm, and Davis and I were able to sit on a bench, overlooking the landscape of the moon Io of Jupiter before us, while Davis, whose conceptual writing preceded that of the so-called Conceptual poets by about seven years, told me of his project in progress, a novel with an envelope of instructions attached to the cover, and at the center of which book would be, in a compartment cut into the pages, a small glass vial of a bio-hazard of some kind, one certain to bring illness to he or she exposed to it, and the instructions would carefully warn the would-be reader that breaking the clasp that sealed the book would, possibly, shatter the poisonous vial that was hidden at the center, thus bringing a sickness (though not necessarily fatal, of course) to the reader, who would, however, thus be able to read the book before experiencing the first symptoms of the poisoning, and then eventually return it, so long as it were within two months of the purchase, dated receipt required, for a full refund of the $20,000 price tag attached to what had been the clasp-sealed artifact. Which I'll refund with no problem, said Davis, Because of the ten that I'll produce, at least two or three will be kept intact by private collectors of conceptual art, and by a couple of folks who just won't want to get sick. And as Davis said this the masses of ice were giving off great reports and retorts, like terrible gunshots, or cannon fire, even, followed by the long, slow shattering of gigantic domes of glass, if that makes any sense. Oh, before I forget, he said, lighting my American Spirit, his hand cupped sub rosa against my face, as if we were lovers, Let me give you your check, and by the way, do you really believe those noises you heard were ghosts *for real*? Boom, went the ice.

I ONCE MET THE MAJOR POET CLAUDIA RANKINE. This was some years ago, at some offsite AWP group reading, though I wasn't part of the group, and I'm not even sure what city it was, now, these blank-outs have begun to shore like flotsam against my backward-looking ruins, maybe it was the MLA. And I wonder as I write this why I have met so very few (as most of what I have recorded in this book reveals) African-American poets, on my occasional jaunts out of the soybean fields. It certainly isn't because I don't want to. Truly, I've always been quite militantly anti-racist, and the major whiteness of the avant poetry field has irked me, indeed, to no end, even if it is, lately, righting itself just a bit, and long live heroic Baltimore. In fact, I don't think I've ever written about this, but before I went to Nicaragua in early 1980, to volunteer as a literacy teacher in the Cruzada de Alfabetización Nacional, one of only three or four U.S. volunteers to do so, actually, and to then return, in 1983, to do the same in the Adult Education campaign, during which time I was in a unit of the Sandinista Militia, in northern Matagalpa, standing against the Reagan Administration's illegal Contra war on the legitimate government of Nicaragua, in which my friend died in a ditch, blood spraying from the stump of his leg, all over me… Before that, I had started off to say, in relation to the topic of race, that I was the Chair of the Student Coalition Against Racism (SCAR) at the University of Wisconsin/Milwaukee, and I was the Presidential candidate for the UWM Student Government on the SCAR ticket, endorsed by the Black Student Union and other progressive groups, and to our surprise we very nearly won, in fact, even though SCAR, no secret to anyone, was a front of the Young Socialist Alliance (YSA), to which I also belonged, itself the youth organization of the communist Socialist Workers Party. And as SCAR's Chair I helped organize numerous forums and rallies, some of them quite large, in defense of busing for school desegregation, of affirmative action, and for corporate and academic disinvestment from South Africa and Namibia, and a good quarter of my comrades in the YSA were African American, and much brighter and more capable, most of them, than I, and they no doubt quietly wondered, within the protocols of Party discipline, why I was Chair, and not one of them, a more than reasonable question, to be sure. And I'm glad I didn't let it all go to my head and go into the State Department's Foreign Service, encouraged by a couple of charming Left-type profs there, no doubt on the CIA role, who were actively wooing me and a few other radicals there, telling us we could surely do more to change things for the better in the State Department, on the inside, where they said our beliefs (with some trimmings) were needed, so, yes, it occurs to me now that maybe that's why I got straight A's in their classes, and there is no question that if I had gone that route I would have ended up as a Progressive Caucus Democrat, like most post-avant poets still are today, in fact, Black and White, or whatever, though not that I've ended up changing things over the past thirty-plus years any more than they have, life is strange. Anyway, I went up to Claudia Rankine, who was not yet famous, while she was talking to a few other poets, a group that included Harryette Mullen, as I recall, and, I think, Joshua Clover, my memory is going, and I told Claudia, whom I hadn't previously met, and who had no idea who I was, I'm sure, how powerful her reading had been, and I thanked her for it, told her I was a fan of her work, and I meant it. She thanked me very warmly for saying so, and then someone else said something to her, and she became distracted, and I went over to say hello to Roberto Tejada, a brilliant poet and critic and the co-editor, with Kristin Dykstra, of the terrific bilingual journal *Mandorla*, where my stuff has appeared a few times. We chatted about some things, Roberto and I, it was all very pleasant and run of the mill, nothing particularly noteworthy. And this entry, I realize now, is somewhat uneventful, too, really, with no twists or surprises or such, unless my transparent attempt above (however true its details) to announce my anti-racist and anti-imperialist record could be regarded as a surprise, which it isn't, since I'm always toiling against my insecurities, doing what I can to make my failures more opaque to others, and without success. So it's a memory of something not all that special, just saying hello to a couple of nice people... But most of life is like that, isn't it, most of the time, people quietly talking, looking around, desiring acceptance and respect, nothing all that remarkable at all.

I once met the remarkable poet Vanessa Place. This was at Princeton, at a symposium on Conceptual Poetry. We were both on the panel, along with Mónica de la Torre, Timothy Donnelly, and Jena Osman. Vanessa vigorously defended Conceptual Poetry, and I expressed my strong skepticism, as did Donnelly, even more than I. Indeed there were a couple moments in the proceedings that seemed a little tense. We all went out to an early dinner at a Turkish restaurant afterwards, and everyone was perfectly civil and protocoled. I talked with my old and genius friend Joshua Kotin, a prof there now, and with my new friend, the Iraq war veteran and writer Roy Scranton, who shortly after was featured on NPR and in the Rolling Stone, and a little bit with some other people, including the poet Ana Božičević, a very nice person, asking them to pass the wine and pepper, and so on. After dinner, in a basement dorm lounge, I gave a warm reading with Sophie Seita and Luke McMullan, two young and stunningly talented poets from England (shortly later I would help arrange the publication of Sophie's first book), though what would happen a year and some months afterwards would be quite different in spirit, alas. A great deal of alcohol was to be found there, as well as at the Nassau Inn Bar later on, where I talked with Orlando Reade, a brilliant doctoral candidate whom I liked very much, indeed, and I went back to my room about 3 AM. The next morning I stumbled upon the station and sat down to wait for the train to Newark. I rubbed my forehead for a long while and then looked up: Why, if it wasn't Vanessa Place, putting her money into the automatic ticket machine! I got up and walked over and said Hello, and she said Hello, and we exchanged cool pleasantries, I suppose is what you could call it, and it was inescapable that we would, in all our poetic animosities, be sitting together on the train for the two-hour ride back to the Newark airport. And so we did… The clatter of the train compounded the near-deafness of my right ear, so that her talking came to me something akin to an erasure of *Paradise Lost*, as erased by Ronald Johnson. Still, it was all courteous enough, and I noticed, from time to time, that she was smiling in a quite friendly way as she spoke in erasures about her recent lecture travels to Denmark and Burma, or wherever, which was interesting, for in all her photographs she doesn't smile at all, of course, nor does she smile in her poetry appearances, apparently, though maybe she does sometimes, I couldn't say for certain, I'm just going from the photographs taken at those, too, and from her delivery at Princeton, which was quite serious, to be sure. I did hear her say that she had missed my reading because she retired early to her room to read a book about Soviet Socialist Realism. I said, Well, I'm an old

Trotskyist, so I don't like Socialist Realism very much. I thought that was mildly clever and funny, in its understated way, but she insisted right away that No, Socialist Realism was, in the end, a fascinating thing, full of possibilities that haven't yet been fully tapped, and I said, raising my voice against the clackety-clack, But who is going to tap them, do you think, Comrade Kenny Goldsmith? And then we arrived at our Finnish station. We took a shuttle, and then an elevator, and then an escalator, and then one of those long treads that roll you a long ways, accompanied by the music of Brian Eno, or by my former roommate from college, Javier Alvarez, who has also written music for airports. Now I could hear her better, and we talked a bit about our respective kids, and the tenderness and poignancy of her remarks were particularly interesting to me, though this part of our passage lasted but fifteen minutes, or so. Then she went to one terminal and I went to another. I'm no less skeptical about the current version of Conceptual Poetry, no less skeptical at all. But I have to say that I came away, really, liking Vanessa Place quite a good bit, life is strange.

I ONCE MET KRISTIN DYKSTRA, whom I mentioned before. This was in Bloomington, Illinois. She is a brilliant translator and scholar, a truly good person. Years later we would edit together a collection in translation of the poems of Amanda Berenguer, about whom I also spoke a few entries above. We were talking in a bar after a reading I gave at Illinois State. Kristin had recently gotten back from Cuba, where she often goes, and I was fascinated to hear about her experience there. I remember we also chatted concerning the *Motorcycle Diaries*, the movie about Ché Guevara in his youth, which we'd both recently seen and liked very much, despite some of the sentimental hagiography. Anyway, Kent, said Kristin, I've brought back some nice news for you from Havana. What's that, Kristin, I said. Well, she said, Have you ever heard of the poet Omar Pérez? No, I hadn't, so she proceeded to tell me he was one of the most prominent poets and essayists of the younger generation, which at the time, years ago, would have meant he was maybe around our age (though that would mean he still is, of course, and always will be), and that he was, amazingly, an ordained Buddhist monk, one of the founders of the very first Zen dojo in the history of Cuba. That's fascinating, I said, with particular curiosity, because long ago I'd edited a big anthology of American Buddhist poetry (as I've previously said), and, too, as a socialist, had long had a keen interest in all things, good and bad, happening inside the Cuban Revolution, and beyond, so to speak, deepened by the fact I'd met a number of good and bad Cuban teachers, doctors, and military trainers during my time in Nicaragua, who told me all sorts of intriguing things about it. Yes, said Kristin, He's an amazing guy and poet, and while I was with him I talked to him about Yasusada and gave him a copy of the book, and he just wrote me a couple days ago to say he's well along into translating a bunch of the poems for publication down there, that he loves the work and the story of it all. I said to Kristin that I was very happy about this, that I would inform Motokiyu right away, and we clinked glasses, and I thanked her, and asked her to have Omar be in touch with me, if he had any questions, and she did ask him that, and it was not too long afterwards that he and I were in touch over email, where he was writing me, oddly, from Holland, where he lived half the year, not something most Cubans in Cuba do, I wondered how that could be. Two weeks later, I think it was, I went to Boston to read in some big assembly hall classroom at MIT, a room filled on most days with people much more intelligent than I, obviously, but on this night there weren't even enough to fill the first two rows of seats, and even then, those who were there were scattered about randomly in the hall, like points in some kind of sad probability field, and after I'd read, one of the people, a poet with whom I'd collaborated on two long poems, came up to me, alcohol on his breath, and started yelling very intensely about Yasusada, inches from my face, and so I walked outside, guarded by the muscular and handsome Dan Bouchard, the editor of the *Poker*, who had invited me there, a true gentleman, and the poet and psychiatrist Mark Weiss, with whom I'd read, came up to me as I lit a cigarette in the chill fall air, and because I was aware he was editing an anthology of Cuban poetry, for Kristin had told me so, I asked him what he knew of Omar Pérez, that I'd heard two weeks back that Omar was translating the poems of Yasusada, and Mark laughed and said, No kidding, how about that? I know Omar, of course, and so does everyone who's anyone in Cuba, given that he's the biological son of Ché Guevara, out of wedlock. Though this last startling fact was something I did not know, until that moment, for Kristin had not revealed it to me, even though she well knew it, Omar not being the sort to want his father advertised as any special feature of his own identity, which as the dharma teaches, as I said on the second page of this book, is illusory anyway, a trace of breeze passing, a mere wisp and apparition, and thus I doubt he would mind my remarking upon it here, revealing a secret that is no secret, a form without form, a truth without truth, so you see what I'm saying, life is strange…

I once met Ben Merriman. This was at the University of Chicago. He is the awesome Fiction Editor of *Chicago Review*, the paramount journal, all in all, of American poetry, though by now, as you read this, he may not be, given how things rotate there. He had written me after reading the furtive edition of my chapbook *I Once Met*, including with the email an imitative sort of prose poem, imagining what it would be like to meet me, how interesting and unusual the encounter would be, and I was struck by how much better, really, his entry was than any of my own. And so I wrote him back to thank him and tell him how much I hoped we would one day, as he imagined, meet. I was reading at the swanky new headquarters of the journal, a building by a hot Japanese architect, and there was a cookout starting on the front lawn, before the event, and Michael Hansen, Andrew Peart, and Nic Wong, the Editor, Poetry Editor, and Non-Fiction Editor, respectively, of *Chicago Review,* three incredibly brilliant young gentlemen, introduced me to Ben, and he said, shyly, Hi, Kent, and I said, Oh, hey, Ben, shyly in return, and we sort of shuffled our feet and cleared our throats and looked at the flames shooting up out of the barbecue, because Joshua Adams, who had just been replaced as Editor, had put too much lighter fluid on the briquettes, and so now there was a kind of bonfire with a big circle of lit-faced people atavistically around it, oohing and aahing, and Ben said, Well, I hope your reading goes well, Kent, and I said, Would you like to have a hamburger together beforehand, or maybe a bratwurst, and Ben laughed, though I'd actually meant it, and said, No, I'm a vegetarian, and then the poets Jill Magi and John Tipton and Yooie Chang came up, and they said hello in the glow of the blue and orange flames, and that was the end of my meeting with Ben, whose chewed fingernails were painted a bright green, I will never forget that, a true gentleman, and whom I hope I will sometime meet again.

I ONCE MET THE FINE POET AND SCHOLAR KASS FLEISHER. This was in Normal, Illinois. She wrote the remarkable book *The Bear River Massacre and the Making of History.* She lives in Normal, where she teaches. Before the reading I was giving there, Kass and her partner, Joe Amato, whom I earlier mentioned, had a pig-roast party, a real one, with the whole pig in the rented roaster, and after the main serving many people were gathered around the pig, picking at its bones, stuffing the meat into their mouths and making dark moaning sounds of delight. I said to Kass, You know, some people, as in certain currents of poets on the coasts, might think this is a bit too unrefined, a bit too primal a manner of dining before a reading, it makes me think of a time I spent shooting guns and such in the forests of southern Ohio, not that I do that often, I've only done it once, actually, I mean in Ohio. I know, said Kass, taking a swig from her can of Bud, But we're here, and we are who we are, and the pig comes from the Schultz's farm, a mile down the road. And then someone young and clearly drunk, whose name I didn't know then, but who would in a few years make a brief reputation for himself as a blogger and attack me with a scathing hatred, took the apple out of the mouth of the mostly eaten carcass and bit deeply into its mushy flesh. Welcome to Normal, I think he said, extending his hand.

I once met the incredible poet from Paraguay, Susy Delgado. This was in Andacollo, Chile, which I've mentioned before. She was generous, witty, genuine, and kind. She has devoted her adult life to bringing Guaraní poetry to a parity of attention with Spanish-language poetry in her country, championing it and its study in her widely read periodical quarterly *Takuapu*, organizing many readings and talks and publications. Her effort has been heroic, and her impact on the contemporary culture of her nation significant. Kent, she said, one night, at the mountain observatory-museum, where in between drinking pisco sours a group of us were giving a reading, to which, somehow, around sixty people had traveled up the mountain, including the mayor and his wife, and two national Congressional representatives, Would you please send me about ten of your poems so I can do a portfolio of them in my journal? Oh, yes, said Silvia Guerra, a major poet of Uruguay, handing me another pisco, *Takuapu* is a very important place, you must! Sure, of course, I said, Thank you very much! And so a year later most of them were published in *Takuapu*, in Asunción, in an issue otherwise mainly devoted to strange, majestic poetry by indigenous writers of Paraguay, old and new, in Guaraní and in Spanish translation, and my frankly less important poems, too, were in Guaraní and Spanish, as rendered by Susy and a young poet, never to be known by you, from the eastern lowlands, the nowhere lands, I have lost the issue and her name. I think those poems stand as my proudest publication ever. I mean, as a poet, I'll take *Takuapu* over places like the *New Yorker,* or *Poetry*, or the *Paris Review*, or what have you, any day. And, prone to hypocrisy though I am, I mean that with all my erratic heart (which I will speak about, in fact, in the next entry).

I ONCE MET THE TREMENDOUS POET QURAYSH ALI LANSANA. He and I have read together twice, in Chicago, and each time we have done so, he has read much better than I, but we all do what we can. He is a true gentleman. At our second meeting, a reading for a book of sestinas we are both in, we greeted one another; I was feeling somewhat not myself, which is not strange to me, as you know by now, but my heart arrhythmia had kicked in a few hours before the reading and wouldn't stop, so I was growing increasingly concerned that this might, indeed, end up being the last poetry reading of my life, an eventuality which would have had both positive and compassionate attributes to recommend it, for sure, but I was, of course, hoping there might still be some other readings to come. Quraysh suggested we sign each other's books, on the pages of our respective entries in the anthology, easy enough to find them, as the contributors were alphabetically arranged. So I gave Quraysh my book and he flipped to the spot, on page whatever, and elegantly signed, with a few kind words of dedication. Then he handed me his copy of the book so that I, familiar with the alphabet, too, might flip to his entry and sign in turn. And I looked at the book and there was the diagram of a spiral on the cover, the kind that people who are passing into the next realm supposedly see and fly into, and I could feel the sweat break out all over me, the palpitations in my chest going off in chaotic percussions, and my mind went blank as a sheet in the morgue: His name had fled my mind, gone poof, nada. I felt panic and began to flip through the big volume, hoping my eyes would alight where they should, but every name was there except his vanished one, for some reason, and so I began to flip faster and faster, saying, Oh, this book is pretty big, isn't it, why do so many damn people write sestinas, or something like that, and I started to do the alphabet thing in my mind, A,B,C,D, E, F, G, etc., hoping the right letter would trigger the last name and save me, but it didn't, and then I closed the book and looked at the great spiral on the cover again, and felt myself sort of falling into it, my heart going through its last, weak premature ventricular contractions, my face hot with fear and shame. And Quraysh put his hand on my shoulder and said, It's Quraysh Ali Lansana, Kent. Did you really forget? And I looked at him, and though I could see some hurt in his eyes, he was also smiling in the gentle way of empathy and forgiveness, and so I went to his pages, at the L's, and signed, and I said, very awkwardly, I am so sorry, Quraysh, you know I know your name, it's my heart, it won't go back to sinus rhythm, and, you know, this puts me in mind of a story a friend once told me, did I ever tell you, Quraysh, about a big formal party, where he began to introduce John

Ashbery to a group of awestruck dignitaries from the Embassy of France, and suddenly he couldn't remember Ashbery's name for the life of him, isn't that funny? Quraysh chuckled politely, and then Daniel Nester came up, and Jenny Boully, and Marissa McNally, and Kathleen Rooney, too, and people dispersed, and thus ended one of the most unforgettable episodes, as it were, of my poetic life.

I ONCE MET JINX NOLAN, and the first name is no typo. This was on my way back to Chicago, connecting with a flight in New York, having come from Sarajevo, Bosnia-Herzegovina, where I'd gone to read from a book of mine translated and soon-to-be published there. I think it was the best trip of my life, and I'll be talking about it more in the next few entries, although then again something happened there between me and my dear friend of years, the one who had forgotten Ashbery's name, and things have never been the same, and I have never understood it, though perhaps there had been something about me to which I'd been blind, and thus I would have no reason to blame him, if the fault was mine, in the end, life is strange. So this would have been 2007. I sat down next to a pleasant looking woman, about my age, maybe a bit older. She was reading the emergency protocol card very intently, and I could tell she was nervous, so I engaged her in conversation, asking her where she was going, the usual. She said Los Angeles, connecting in Chicago, and that she wasn't looking forward to the next seven hours, or whatever, because she was terrified of flying. I told her that I hated flying, too, white knuckles all the way, only did it when I had to. She asked me why I flew and when I had to. I said it was usually when I was invited to a poetry reading, wherever, though it didn't happen very often, in any case, so I only had to confront my phobia, really, a couple desperate times a year, at most. I expected her to smile politely at this, maybe even gently laugh, but she looked at me sternly and said, as if telling me something grave I didn't already know, or regret: *You are a poet.* I sensed that she meant the apparent accusation as a kind of question, so I said, Yes, I'm afraid so, or said something like that. Oh, she said, Did you know that my father is Sidney Nolan, Australia's most famous artist, and that he painted, back in the 1940s, when he was close to the Angry Penguins, the famous portrait of Ern Malley, who is Australia's most famous Modernist poet, though he really didn't exist, I wonder if you know about Ern Malley, since you are a poet? The engines roared, and the plane began to roll. What?? I said... I said, she said loudly, That Sidney Nolan, my father... No, no, I shouted, It's just that I can't believe this! What? she said, turning her head this way and that, What can't you believe? Is something wrong?? *What's wrong, my God!!* The impossible plane lifted impossibly into the sky, and we both sat back and shut our eyes to die, life is strange. By and by, when the attendants were walking by, indicating immediate crisis had passed, I said to her, opening my cashews, You know, what I meant before, when I said I can't believe this, is that I've been a huge fan of Ern Malley for many years, and I have been involved myself in a work that has been very controversial in ways at least partly similar to Ern Malley, though it's also very different, of course: the work of Araki Yasusada… What?? she said. I began to repeat what I'd said, but she cut me off: *Are you Kent Johnson?!* Yes, that is me, I said, popping a nut into my mouth, which had more or less fallen open all by itself. My name is Jinx Nolan, she said, extending her hand. Jinx? I said. Yes, Jinx, I know it sounds like a typo, or something, my father's sense of humor extended to the naming of his children, and I am on my way to Los Angeles to settle a suit over the authentic ownership of my father's estate, which has more or less been stolen from me, and against my father's true wishes, who never had the chance to properly complete his will…and you have to admit it's pretty strange that we should be sitting next to each other, 30,000 feet up in the air, or whatever, I am feeling very afraid. I nodded my vigorous agreement. But tell me about your father's estate, I said, What is this all about? She was happy to talk about it, and did so in finest detail and in nervous earnestness, covering the most obscure meanderings of the legal intrigue, and she did so nearly non-stop, all the way to Chicago, for nearly two hours. I remember almost nothing of the details, though I learned, a year or so later, from the exceptional Australian poet John Tranter, that she had lost the case and was crushed over the matter. The seat belt sign came on and we began to go down. As we did, the weather got bad, and the plane began to bounce and buck about, alarmingly. She reached for my hand and locked her fingers into mine, as if we were a couple, on our suicide bed. We put our heads back and shut our eyes… When we landed (how does it happen?), she of course let go of my hand (wiping the sweat, I noticed, quickly, on her slacks), and a kind of normal-life awkwardness settled between us. The plane taxied to the gate. We got up, like all people, to get our luggage out of the bin. Well, good luck with the case, I said, I wish you the best in Los Angeles. She looked at me and said she couldn't believe the matters of Ern Malley and Yasusada had ended up sitting together, in coach, or something mildly funny like that. And, she said, I can't believe, either, that I went on so long as I did, you can see it has been weighing on my mind, and I never even got you to talk about Yasusada, but do you have a card, and we can stay in contact over email? No? OK, well, here's mine, please write me so we can be in touch. Goodbye, I said. Goodbye, she said. Good luck! I said. And the same to you! she said. I looked down, in the airport van, at the top of my hand, where the marks of her nails still showed, as faint signs of a bluish red, like an ancient tattoo from the dreamtime. And that this is all true is stranger to me than it could be to you, whoever, or wherever, you may be.

I once met the splendid poet Dijala Hasanbegović. This was 2007. She was in charge of the seven-citied Sarajevo Poetry Days conference. The night I arrived, Dijala and her friend Mladen Vuković had insisted that, You must stay up! You must stay up to avoid the jet-laggings! So after stopping by a couple bars, a group of us found ourselves at 3 AM in a bookstore-café called Buy Book… Against better wisdom, exhausted to the point of waking dream, but enjoying it immensely, I smoked, for smoking is the national sport in Bosnia, and that is the moment where I picked up the habit again, for the next six and a half years. As we left, I heaved my book-filled bag to sling it on my shoulder and hit Dijala behind me, hard, knocking the breath from her small body. She crouched down for about half a minute, gasping. I'm so sorry, Dijala, I said, again and again, mortified. That's OK, she said, slowly rising and taking a shaky light from Mladen, In Bosnia, two kidneys is a bonus, don't you know. A lovely, gracious woman.

I once met the blue-chip poet Pedja Kojović. He has translated, with Azra Radaslić, my book *Lyric Poetry after Auschwitz*, along with other poems, for publication in Bosnia and Croatia. On my second night in Sarajevo, Pedja rolled cigarettes for everyone from his tobacco pack, for what's on the table, as the Bosnian saying goes, is for the table. The editor, with the renowned Semezdin Mehmedinović, of the publishing house Ajfelov Most Books, he showed me on his laptop the plans and layouts of my book, all in fine and cutting-edge design. Handsome, roguish, quick of wit, Pedja was, in his early twenties, one of Reuters' crack combat photographers during the Balkan war, and he had seen a great deal in his thirty-some years. Years after that war, when Saddam Hussein was taken from his "rat hole" outside Baghdad, he was there, to take the very first images as the tyrant peered up, filthy and forlorn, through the trap door at his captors. You have seen it, life is strange. This is going to be a wonderful and important poetry series we will do, guys, just you wait and see. We aim to be the New Directions in this corner of the world! Applause from the table.

I once met the marvelous poet Elvis Mujanović. This was in Sarajevo. A shy, melancholic young man, he was assigned to be my interpreter during the conference there. Over nine days together, an unusual closeness developed between us. On the first day, drinking coffee in the hotel, overlooking the city, getting to know a bit about each other, he told me of his family in the western town of Cazin, how during the war it was taken over by a breakaway faction of the Bosnian forces and became the site of terrible intra-Muslim fighting. Imagine the desperation and shame we felt, and always the fear that we would die for nothing, he said. He told me how his mother, a fan (it goes without saying) of Elvis Presley, and a heavy smoker, would hoard all her cigarettes as currency to purchase basic provisions for the family, eating, of the little she could get, almost nothing herself. But he and his two sisters would steal one or two cigs from each pack and store them away to give to their mom to smoke when her depression would grow especially strong. The house gets hit by a shell one day, when they are, for some reason, not there. Relatives and friends die, as soldiers or bystanders. A rotting horse swells to the size of a hippo and bursts all over the road. Medieval buildings collapse into rubble. An old man, driven mad by grief, calmly walks a cat on a rope, as the firefight proceeds around him. Famished dogs snarl over the entrails of the maggot-covered hippo-horse. We were quiet for a while. Traffic sounds and school-kid laughter, shouts of daily commerce below the balcony. And then he lit a cigarette, asked me about my own family, do my parents still live, am I married, do I have children, etc.

I ONCE MET MARIO HIBERT. He was a young, decorated sharpshooter with the Bosnian resistance during the war. He is a deeply gifted poet and critic, now a Ph.D. and professor, and I will always remember him as one of the kindest, deepest persons I have met in my life. On the morning I left Sarajevo to get back for final exams, Mario, emotionally, pressed into my hand a small thing. It is for your journey, he said, A modest gift from my wife Monja and me, a little memory… It was a key ring, with a piece of polished pine attached, and on it, a verse from the Koran, in miniature Arabic, that he himself had burned, with a stylus, into the wood. And we embraced and cried, for a short while. It is still with me, wherever I go. I've put it in the rubber bin, where you put your change and shoes and wallet and whatnot, when you go through the scanner, and no one has stopped me, yet. May the love of Allah accompany you forever. Goodbye, Kent, my friend. Goodbye, Mario, my friend.

I ONCE MET THE WORLD-FAMOUS WRITER CÉSAR AIRA. This was in Buenos Aires, where Forrest Gander and I were giving a reading, following a visit to Uruguay. I know I've mentioned Forrest a few times already, but we've traveled to seven or eight countries together, so it's natural that I should. Aira met us at his favorite bookstore, a terrific place, and we poked around there for an hour or so, while he showed us different books he liked and talked a bit about each one, especially those of Bolaño, Borges, Piglia, and Pizarnik. A couple people there came up and asked him to sign copies of his own titles, which he did, with flourishing hand. We walked, then, some blocks through Palermo, one of the city's old beautiful neighborhoods, and he pointed out the house where Borges grew up, which has a prominent plaque, and then we went to a bar, a writer's spot, he told us, and sat down at a sidewalk table, and I could see that a number of people at other tables began to look his way and comment to each other, which made sense, given that this was apparently a literary hangout, and Aira is the most famous living writer of Argentina. We sat there for three beers, or so, in the evening sun, Forrest and I asking him this and that about his work; the weather was temperate, and it was a very pleasant chat. He had been talking about chance and the unsuspected divagations in fiction that unfold beyond the writer's command, even when the writer endeavors to edit and control the forces of chance, for even in doing so chance will simply make itself known again and again, popping up through the wormholes of Being that the signs of writing proffer – that chance, in fact, is the very heart of fiction in the deepest orders of its measureless office (he then made a pun on the word orifice), orders that have nothing to do with literary form, in fact, which is merely phantasmal in any case, and a forgery of the gods, to make us feel better about ourselves, or so I best recall him saying. And so then I said to Aira and Forrest that something had happened to me just that very morning, when I was with the video artist and writer Leticia El Halli Obeid, at another café in Palermo, going over translations that she had been doing of my poetry, and which were soon coming out in Spain, which of course was flattering to me. I said that what had happened to me then was certainly the most bizarre and impossible series of happenstances that had ever visited me in my life, that I was still feeling quite dazed about the near-occult nature of it, life is strange, and that the events had put Leticia, too, into a state of shocked astonishment, and so I proceeded to recount what had taken place, and I'll skip over relating it all here, because if I did it would come off as so unlikely that the credibility of this entire book of actual memories, so to speak, would be thoroughly undermined. And when

I'd finished, both Forrest and Aira sat there gazing at me, with dumbfounded faces, for about seven seconds, until Aira burst out laughing, a great and long aria of guffaw which he accompanied with the loud clapping of hands. And he thanked me, effusively, for telling the story, said it was truly memorable, a reminder that a whole dimension of quantum strangeness most certainly waited for moments of entanglement with diffident smirk and bearing behind our own dimension, which is – our dimension, that is – a kind of "ontological dementia," as he surprisingly termed it, in the gnostic sense of it all, and that the clarity and purity of the former seeps through, now and then, for whatever reason, into the banal forgetfulness of the latter, and that this seeping, in its punctuated episodes, is what we usually call coincidence or, even, the uncanny, but that its more intense and extended manifestations, such as what I had recounted, are what we know as magic or transcendence, and that what had happened to me and Leticia and the other three people involved was clearly of this last, this pure kind, without a doubt. And then he laughed some more, and so did we, and after a time of sitting there quietly, each of us just thinking and looking about, Forrest and Aira turned to talking a bit about practical details concerning Forrest's translation of one of Aira's novels. And at a certain point, without any warning whatsoever, and which somehow came off as a perfectly elegant gesture, for any elegant gesture is by nature a surprise, Aira said, Well, I'm off! and he got up, shook hands, and walked, feminine and tough, away down the street. Around two months later, I think it was, Forrest sent me an email, in which he told me he'd just had a letter in which Aira referred to the strange experience I'd recounted that day and that Aira told him he had taken the outlines of it and made it the opening of the novel or novella he was currently writing. But to my knowledge, this novel or novella has not yet appeared.

I ONCE MET THE MASTERFUL EDITOR ERIC LORBERER. This was in Minneapolis. He is the founder of the marvelous magazine *Rain Taxi,* a wonderful man, a true gentleman. He invited me to give a lecture and reading at the Walker Arts Center, and so I, of course, did just that. I spent the afternoon there walking on the bridge that carries, inscribed upon it, a poem by John Ashbery and also wandering around the big retrospective at the Walker of the conceptual artist Richard Prince, who a few years from then would carry in his NYC book gallery a rare copy of my DAY, offering it for a price tag exceeding the price of Kenneth Goldsmith's version by two zeroes, which I've always thought was an original touch, as they say. But as I was looking at paintings of zombie nurses and faked de Koonings and poached photos of the Marlboro Man, an ice storm began to fall, and it quickly became one of the worst ice storms in Minneapolis for many a season, coating, now, the trees and cars and statues in two inches of gleaming glass, making the whole city a kind of vast conceptual apparition decided by the sky that no appropriation artist could ever reproduce. And with the ice still falling, there were around forty people who somehow, unaccountably, made it to my event, which really should have been cancelled, and I looked at them, in the lecture hall, as they clapped to welcome me, in the friendly Nordic way, and I thought, more with a sudden feeling of ontological wonder than with any sense of well-justified self-deprecation: What on Earth are they doing here?

I've never met Emily Dickinson, whom I've previously mentioned, though if there were a time machine, and I could choose whom to bring back, I think it would be her. Yes, if she and Da Vinci and Wittgenstein and Spinoza and Whitman and Christ and C.L.R James and Cervantes and Buddha and Shakespeare and Basho and Crazy Horse and Sappho and Holiday and Danton and Dalton and Paine and Lincoln and King and Mirabai and Coltrane and Di Giorgio and Guevara and Partch and Baraka and Marx and Lady Murasaki and Vallejo and Lorca and Woolf and Trotsky and Mozart and Tupac Amaru and Catullus and Duchamp and Durruti and Kahlo and Rublev and Malevich and Rumi and Picasso and Baudelaire and Beatrice and Poe and Debs and Mother Jones and Ho Chi Minh and Niedecker and Wang Wei and Baldwin and Saenz and O'Hara and Du Bois and Al-Khansa and Clare and Smart and Jefferson and Langston Hughes and Pizarnik and Li Bo and Tubman and Villon and Le Corbusier and Frank Lloyd Wright and Elizabeth I and Artigas and Akiko Yosano and Bolaño and Borges and Bishop and Gaudí and H.D. and Césaire and Dōgen and Sequoyah and Dante and Smithson and Plato and Augustine and Mayakovsky and Agustini and Averroes and Douglass and Osceola and Jonson and Sor Juana and Akhmatova and Malcolm X and Luxemburg and Pessoa, just for example, were in a long lineup from which I was to choose just one to spend a weekend with at a Sandals Resort in the Bahamas, it would have to be with Emily Dickinson. I have shamelessly imagined her in a bikini, stretched out by the pool, oiled and sweaty, sipping a mojito, staring at paunchy, pear-shaped me over her sunglasses, casually sharing, in a high and dulcet voice, the fathomless mysteries of her impossible mind.

Doggerel for the Masses

Which is a problem, I suppose

They've shut me out, I'll never win.
They keep on quoting Silliman.[1]
The youth's been trained, they know the show:[2]
Ignore the Out and praise the In.
I never meant to end this way!
It all goes back to Buffalo.[3]

I think I'll just collect my stamps,
My books and stuff, my lava lamps.[4]
The institution has its rules.
The slavish win, the gadflies lose.
It didn't always have that twist,
But now it does, old Trotskyist.[5]

---

[1] Or at least they used to when he was blogging. The background impulse for the quotation, of course, was usually the hope (almost always borne out) that Silliman would see his name in Google Alert and then link to the post, in evident desire to extend his cultural capital.

[2] Grammatically, that should really be the youth *have* been trained. But meter rules.

[3] See the Buffalo Poetics List Archives for the second half of 1998 and my appraisal of the demise of the List at http://www.flashpointmag.com/skanky.htm

[4] I have an actual collection of lava lamps, along with complete and expanding collections of Ugly Duckling Presse and Brian Teare's Albion Books. As it turns out, these are the only things of value I own, in the end, to leave my two sons.

[5] I was a member of the Socialist Workers Party for over ten years in the seventies and eighties, during much of which time I quit school to do trade-union work for the Party as a freight-car mechanic on the now-defunct Milwaukee Road. I could say a lot more about my Trotskyist past, including accounts of battle experience fighting the Contras in Nicaragua as part of the local Sandinista Militia (with an old Czech BZ rifle, a model infamous for regular jamming), where I taught literacy in the mountains for a total of fourteen months in 1980 and 1983, acute dysentery the first time, typhoid the second. O, the world has changed, that's for sure. But what hasn't changed, apparently, is that I do enjoy talking about myself…

I can't believe it's come to this:
The wish to kiss the Mainstream ass.[6]
You have to kneel to gain success;
To Perloff, Burt, or Adam Kirsch.
It's how you get in *Poetry*:[7]
Politeness is maturity.

Don't think I can't give head like you;
I'm compromised, no less than you.
I'm weird because I place my face
In your despise, to spite my nose.
I don't know what the hell that means.
Which is a problem, I suppose.

---

[6] The "Mainstream" is not what it used to be.

[7] Poetry magazine, where the CIA and NSA have put their money, figuratively (perhaps) speaking. Also appendage of the Poetry Foundation, a $100,000,000 Big-Pharma-funded culture corporation that calls the cops on young poets who exhibit true a-g spirit and then urges judges to send them to places like the violence-ridden Cook County Correctional Facility. Of course, most "post-avantists," eager to show "professional" decorum as good citizens of the Poetic Field (the young bureaucrats at the Poetry Foundation are helping to keep track!), have kept a careful silence about the latter. This footnote connects to footnote #6 of "If poetry's to hit the mark."

And when cell rings, my legs blow off

The thing I'm trying to explain
Is that it's all a suicide,
This crap of iambs that would be
Some statement of acuity,
Is all a mess of self-regard,
The measure's in my ego drive.

I want to strap a belt to me,
To blow up my hypocrisy.
I ask my comrade Christian Bök,
To set it off with Blackberrý;
But he declines preoccupied,
With microbes and eternal fame. [1]

I call up my friend Marjorie
And ask her if she'll help poor me.
I ask her will she detonate
The belt I wear on my midriff.
But she says No, says back to me,
She's with Death Condie in Hong Kong. [2]

---

[1] Bök is implanting a DNA poetic code of sorts into a bacterium; as he readily admits, he hopes his work will live for billions of years beyond the extinction of the human race.

[2] Condoleeza Rice, former President of Stanford University and Secretary of State in the Bush Administration, one of the principal architects of the concocted mass-murder war in Iraq and a close friend of Marjorie Perloff, critical champion of the American Language and Conceptual poets. If this suggests I don't hold Marjorie Perloff in great esteem, the wrong impression is given. Though I was the first (in a 2013 *Chicago Review* article) to publicly lambast her for retrograde racialist atmospheres fogging her criticism, she has been a prolifically brilliant critic and equally prolific in her generous support of poets and critics far and wide. See the reference to Perloff in the poem before this one. Ideology is complicated.

I write my fan, the man at Penn,
I ask him if he'll help me out.
He closely listens to my plan,
And promises to call right back.
And I say Yes, Charles, thank you much.
And when cell rings, my legs blow off. [3]

---

[3] Though I've only spoken once to Charles Bernstein in person (in company of the late, great Carl Rakosi, in Orono, Maine, quite a good number of years ago), I hope we will have another opportunity. He's claimed (in a book published in 2011 by University of Chicago) that because of my ties to the Yasusada affair I am a racist who is driven by "White Male Rage."

But poetry exceeds her world

You think that satire's all I got,
Though you don't know the half of it.
I don't proclaim to be *Fence* stuff,
But grief for Nancy Smith was rough,[1]
For me and friends and all the sheep,
Who baa with faces of our dead.[2]

I do respect the New York School,
The Language folks, Projectivists;
I do admire Hybrid stuff,
The San Francisco Renaissance.
My nag is with the burning girl,
Who screams in iambs for Allah.

Though then I go to latte shop,
And order there a fancy drink.
I gaze out on the Brooklyn scene
And read my homey, Kenneth Koch.[3]
When John comes by we say hello,
We share our versions from Rimbaud.[4]

---

[1] "Grief for Nancy Smith": lifted from a long poem by John Ashbery. It was in APR; I can't recall the title.

[2] Some may sense an allusion here to my poem about John Ashbery, James Tate, Dean Young, and myself, the one titled "The Best American Poetry," but there is no allusion.

[3] One of my favorite poets, totally underestimated, possibly to be seen as the Alexander Pope of our times, though it's not yet the time.

[4] Both Ashbery and I have translated Rimbaud's *Illuminations*, my own done with Kenny Goldsmith, Christian Bök, Kasey Silem Mohammed, and Vanessa Place, under the collective name of "The Rejection Group."

Our talk gets dark, we deeply kiss,
We fondle each one's private parts.
We don't get hard because we're old,
But hand jobs beat limp politics.
The girl is ash, and that's a shame,
But poetry exceeds her world.

Of Concept and Imperium

It is a triumph, let's proclaim,
For our Conceptual Poetry,
To be invited by Michelle,[1]
As drones buzz over Pakistan,
To read to children poetry,
Of Whitman, Crane, and traffic jams.

It's not quite clear why there's a fuss,
That some complain as if it's wrong,
For we all do fill up our cars,
With gas that comes from our allies.
Such sour grapes provide a laugh,
At M-L-A and Orono.

You can't experiment at ease,
Without the concept that we're One,
With oil and coal and weapons sales;
They give you your career and books,
Your conferences, your whip, and thong,
Your drinks, your pot, your lexicon.

---

[1] In May, 2011, Kenny Goldsmith read at the White House with Billy Collins and some other poets. The reading was introduced by the President of the United States. Mr. Goldsmith wore an extravagant bowtie and fancy suit; he slavishly praised Obama and the First Lady in his introductory remarks. This sorry kowtowing to the Imperial State was prominently praised as a great honor for the American "avant-garde" on the home page of *Jacket2*.

Let's give a cheer to our Kenný
For he has placed us in our place,
Which is the place of our estate,
To be at last within the State, [2]
For there's no break between the lines,
Of Concept and Imperium.

---

[2] Literally.

The bids go wack at *Jacket2*

It tears me down, my friends are few.
It pains my heart, the farm's come down.
The tools are sold, the flock long gone.
The plow's in scrap, the car no more.
It tears me down, my friends are few.
It pains my heart, this denouement.[1]

It drives me wild, this sell-out field.
It fries my brains, the die is cast.
Ed Dorn is dead, and dear Lorine.[2]
The auction's packed, the hands go up.
It tears me down, it's all for sale.
It pains my balls, this "avant-garde."

---

[1] This is autobiography. I am lonely, sad, and grossly overweight, suffering from a case of psoriasis whose epidermal effects are as acute as those of leprosy, and this, no doubt, accounts for the poem's dark mood.

[2] Lorine Niedecker, of Fort Atkinson, Wisconsin, a town (not least its bars) I know better than any other post-avant poet does. Not that Dorn and Niedecker are pure, that's for sure: Dorn infamously displayed a mean homophobic streak (result, perhaps, as so often the case, of latent homosexual drives?); and the purported saintly Niedecker begins a poem written a fortnight after the bombing of Hiroshima with this atavistic bit of anti-Semitism, perhaps releasing pent-up anger at Louis Zukofsky, who pressured her into aborting their illegitimate child:

> **New**
>
> **Reason explodes. Atomic split**
>
> **shows one element**
>
> **Jew**

The birds are white, the birds are black.
The streams once fished are shined in scum.
The Language poets thrill the Profs.
It's gone to seed, what will you do?
Fine cock's been sucked and tenure's come.
You can't go back to Paterson.

I'd try myself, but I give up.
They've got the youth and they have won.
It's all arranged in rows and ranks.[3]
It kills my heart, this auction house.
It tears me down, my friends are few.
The bids go wack at *Jacket2*.

---

[3] An allusion to the schoolroom, where students sit obediently, albeit acting up now and then, something the school certainly expects, even encourages, as part of the professional indoctrination process.

And here, old man, you'll never be

We feel your pain, your satire's lost,
Amidst the hybrid elegance.
It's sad you just don't have the stuff,
To make it to the Norton thing[1]
If you'd but stop your pompous crap,
You might befriend a few of us.

We're smart and keen, you can't blame us:
We've paid our dues, high school was tough.
The nerds that were are now the froth;[2]
We're not about to shout and huff.
We'll leave that to the malcontents,
Who don't know how to play the Field.[3]

This is your lack, this cluelessness,
About how nimbleness doth work;
You claim it's all a sellout thing,
But our dance moves are difficult.[4]
Why don't you check your O-So-Wise,
Grow up and institutionalize?[5]

---

[1] *American Hybrid*, the logical, historically inevitable follow-up to Paul Hoover's Norton anthology, *Postmodern American Poetry*.

[2] This fact has perhaps more impact on the mean, cliquish politics of the avant poetry world than is acknowledged.

[3] See Pierre Bourdieu on the Cultural Field and the agonistic taking of positions by its actors.

[4] A delayed compensation. See footnote 2.

[5] "tional": read as elided.

The Pulitzer has now been won,
The N-B-A and on and on.
There's not been such since Allen Tate
Laid down the law that makes us free.[6]
You can complain, but we are here,
And here, old man, you'll never be.

---

[6] This is perhaps my greatest pair of lines in this book of sestets. But it's best left without " clarification."

If poetry's to hit the mark

Farid explodes and that's too bad; [1]
Our work's now read in Allahbad.
That makes us feel a bit confused,
But this doth swell avantist muse.
You take your oil from where it comes.
We wish to win a Major Prize. [2]

The culture's mowed, what is our place?
We seem to be a lumpen race.
Reduced to games of fraud and theft, [3]
And readings for the C-I-A. [4]
It could be worse, we could be dead,
Like bride and groom on some lost road.

---

[1] This is not a reference to the American poet Farid Matuk.

[2] In just the past few years, American post-avantists have won the Pulitzer Prize, two National Book Awards, two National Book Critics' Circle Awards, a Lenore Marshall Prize, a couple Griffin Prizes, a couple MacArthur Grants, about two dozen Guggenheims and National Endowment for the Arts awards, a star turn at the White House, three or four guest appearances on the PBS NewsHour, and scores of other prominent institutional prizes and honors, not to mention major publications with mainline commercial and university presses (especially Ivy League ones) and legitimating journals and anthologies (such as *Poetry*, the *New Yorker*, various Nortons, Penguins, etc). The post-avant, solidly ensconced in the Academy (with scores and plus of tenure-track positions, Associate Professorships, and Corporate-funded Chairs, not to mention a whole secondary layer of industrious critics and grad students whose careers, present and future, are tied to studies of these poets), still regards itself as an embattled "opposition."

[3] A reference to the stated aims of Conceptual Poetry, as articulated by its leading spokespeople.

[4] The immediate reference is obvious. The more secondary allusion is to the CIA's active sponsorship in the fifties and sixties of the export of U.S. avant-garde art, namely Abstract Expressionism, as part of its overall international propaganda strategy.

Let's count our stars, though small they be;
We can't expect celebrity. [5]
Our fraud and theft, though, is enough,
To get in bed with John R. Barr,
Who calls the State on leftist bards,
Though we'll ignore that, times are tough. [6]

We are behind the Art World's eyes,
By fifty years, some more besides. [7]
We must catch up with Warhol's cans,
Or with Judd's thing at D-I-A. [8]
Our Author Function must drone up, [9]
If poetry's to hit the mark.

---

[5] Relatively speaking. Attention's on the rapid rise. It's sort of like a collegial Parliament now. Like the Green Party in Germany, or something. Though more like the Democratic Party in the U.S., really…

[6] John Barr (I don't know if R. is his middle initial, but it will do for the meter), a multimillionaire investment banker, has been President of the Poetry Foundation since 2004, charged with managing *Poetry* magazine's $100 million gift from Ruth Lilly, the late and eccentric pharmaceutical industry heiress. The reference to "leftist bards" concerns the eight young poets and artists of the Croatoan Poetic Cell who carried out two peaceful protest actions (the second at the reading of the great Chilean poet and rebel CADA activist Raúl Zurita) at the 20+ million Poetry Foundation headquarters building in Chicago during September of 2011. The PF called the cops on the CPC activists, most of whom scampered away. One of them, Stephanie Dunn, was tackled by PF Security Guards, blocked from leaving the building, handcuffed by the police on their arrival, and taken to jail (she reports suffering pornographic sexual harassment there) at the lyrical request of the PF representatives. Approximately three weeks later, at her court hearing, the PF sent two official reps to demand before the judge that Dunn be locked up in the Cook County Penitentiary – a violence-ridden hell hole – pending her trial eight days later. In the wake of these events, the CPC put up two statements at Montevidayo blog, explaining these events and protesting the PF's obscene siccing of the State on other poets, guilty of nothing but modest civil disobedience actions in perfect keeping with venerable avant-garde tradition. The great majority in the American "post-avant" poetry world knew about these posts (as well as subsequent feature articles

about the matter in major publications like the *Chicago Reader* and *Salon*), and it is of special note that only a few of its denizens chose to speak publicly in response, even after Zurita had gone on record expressing his "profound tenderness" for the CPC commandoes. This timid, opportunist-tinged refusal to protest such base violation of poetic-ethical principles will come to be seen, I am convinced, as one of the most shameful episodes in the history of 21st century American poetry.

[7] A claim often made by Conceptual poets, who nevertheless keep rehearsing moves made in the art world fifty years or more before.

[8] Donald Judd, whose Minimalist sculpture is installed at the DIA center in Marfa, Texas, where many big-name "experimental" poets go on retreat, with grants from hedge-fund monies.

[9] See Michel Foucault's classic essay, "What Is an Author?"

You'll let us sell you avant-garde

We're on our way, fair Wichita.
We're coming soon, dear Idaho.
We've got far Burma, the Chinese,
The Argentines, the Portuguese.
Old Satire's dead and that's a fact.
We'll have our branch in Vanderbilt.[1]

We're on our way, Sewanee rag.
We're coming soon, Ohio mag.[2]
They thought the *Nation*'d never fall,[3]
New Yorker's, even, coming round.[4]
And if you thought tenacity
Was lacking in our tenure drive:

Well, take a look at *Poetry*,[5]
At Brown, and Harvard, Princeton, Penn,[6]
The Wops, the Ruskies, and the Frogs,
The Polacks, Krauts, Canadians,
And laugh with mirth at Satirist,
Who moans away pathetic'ly…

---

[1] There are some complicated things going on here.

[2] Allusions: T*he Sewanee Review*, one of the last holdouts of the New Critical/Confessional mash-up of the sixties. Likewise the *Ohio Review*, one of the last holdouts of the Confessional/Deep Image mash-up of the late sixties and seventies.

[3] Peter Gizzi became Poetry Editor of the *Nation* in 2007; Jordan Davis succeeds him.

[4] Numerous post-avantists (most notably the neo-minimalist Rae Armantrout) have been published there, some repeatedly.

[5] No explanation seems necessary.

We're coming soon, sweet Uruguay,[7]
We're on our way Afghanistan,
And if they block us in Riyadh,
We'll point to Goldsmith's *Capital*,[8]
And say that if you want our bonds,
You'll let us export avant-garde.

---

[6] Academic centers of post-Language poetry: the new Kenyons and Vanderbilts.

[7] The native land of Lautréamont, where I grew up, between 1961 and 1971, and to where I returned in 1977 through '78.

[8] The title of his latest book, a rewriting of Walter Benjamin, perhaps the saddest thing in poetry since Robert Duncan was denied publication in the *Kenyon Review* for being homosexual.

His arm's blown off; he weeps clown tears

The Language poets did once write
Of Capital and Reference.
But now they sit in special Chairs,
Whose Names denote Imperium.[1]
It's not that I presume to blame;
There's Bürger who explained the game.[2]

Bourdieu did too, though he's passé;[3]
You'll never find him on PENN Sound.
Baraka sits in his dotáge,
Bug-eýed and clear about some things.
Though certainly he's queer to think
That Bush had known it all along.[4]

As are the Arabs who did dance
When Towers fell in tragedy.
Our youth dance too, in black revenge,[5]
What is the role for poetry?
Though I don't claim to know the key,
It's not the University!

---

[1] Check it out. Never in the history of American poetry has there been such a lineup of heavy iron crowns of irony.

[2] Peter Bürger: See his classic study *Theory of the Avant-Garde*.

[3] Pierre Bourdieu. See works related to the Cultural Field of Production.

[4] Amiri Baraka, profoundly great American poet, homophobe and anti-Semite of record, who suggested 9/11 was a Zionist plot.

[5] In the early morning hours, after the execution of Osama bin Laden. See the "Song of Despair" at the end of this sequence.

Of this I'm sure, I swear by Brecht,
Rukéyser, Olson, Levertov,
Rimbaud, Vallejo, and Hikmet! [6]
They seem so quaint now, in our Field.
The child goes running through the field,
His arm's blown off, he weeps clown tears.[7]

---

[6] Etc. etc, they who would have hammered the first stray piece of metal found into a rough spoon so to gouge out their eyes had they seen what has happened to our sell-out poetic "avant-garde."

[7] Take your pick from among thousands of much more horrific scenes. How's your microbrew?

The Ivy League, the NSA

I dare they put this on PENNSound;
I know they won't, but I lay down
The challenge that they do at last
Include me in menagerie.
For surely they do not make choice
Contingent on mere politics!

I'm sure they don't, I'm sure they're fair,
That paranoia gropes my brain,
And their M.O.'s aesthetical,
A matter of what's fine or not,
And anyway, why should they care
About my silly metered shit?[1]

Of course I'm wrong in my unease,
To think that it's all just a game,
Of who's in power, who is not,
For poetry's immune to such,
And ethics rise towards the sky,
And make its dome a rosy hue.

---

[1] Actually, my "metered shit" is not so silly: It would be nice to see post-avant poets show they can write in traditional forms, which are, after all, to our trade what the ability to draw, at least with rough competence, is to the realm of painting. Most younger "post-avant" poets, in fact, have taken convenient, professionally driven shortcuts into easy mannerist abstraction, or into easy mannerist conceptualism. Maybe "tachism" is a better word than "mannerism." This is not to blame *them*. It's a system.

Where all the pettiness dissolves
Like in a Frederick Church landscape,
Which leads to Ashcan School and thén
To flatter things in Greenberg's creed,[2]
The things craved by the M-L-A,
The Ivy League, the N-S-A![3]

---

[2] Clement Greenberg. While old-guard Langpo is still largely stuck in basic Greenbergian/Adornean categories (not that the categories of these two thinkers are identical, but they are contiguous in important ways), I do realize certain currents of post-Langpo have struggled to free themselves from such (the turn to high-theory flirtations with "kitsch," neo-Dada cut-paste-and-slash, and post-Pop Warholian reproduction, etc.). Nevertheless, they've never been able to make the final and necessary move to autonomous space. Indeed, the ground institutional habitus (the Academy, evidently) from which their work emanates is blithely assumed as natural by nearly all these belated "Neo-neo-avant-garde" writers.

[3] The National Security Agency, which under the "progressive" Obama Administration has gained unprecedented power and undermined fundamental Constitutional principles. One can be quite sure it is already helping to promote the "export" of our experimental poetry to neo-colonial hotspots as evidence of our "advanced" culture. That's a lot of "inverted commas"!

End of the War on Terror[1]

We have taken custody of his body.
In this spell of intimacy, may our sins seem washed away.
For look: Thousands of youths with phones mass in flash
    release:
They bear flags; they scale trees; they stand, pushed up,
    balancing
on the hands of their companions. They're astonished to be
    living it.
Sudden shot on the screen: Two boys leap into the air, again
and again, crash ecstatically against the chest of the other.
    Someone's
beautiful daughter breaks away, runs screaming towards the
    lens,
thumbs up, tongue out, in a kind of ululation.
Try to understand us. See we share your fears, desires,
dreams. Poetry matters to us in same measure it matters
    to you.
It has been this way, and so it will. Deep grief and joy, great
    pleasure
and pain get fused; who can tell, sometimes, the difference
    on the face?
Anchorman asks a guest on Skype: "He has been called
the very face of Evil… You who lost your father in the
    tower on
that terrible day, how does this historic moment make
    you feel?"

---

[1] Written the day after Obama's midnight announcement. Certainly one of the first poems written in the U.S. about the death of Osama bin Laden.

"O," he says, "It's hard to find the words. At first I was
   so happy,
and then I felt guilty, all of a sudden, to be celebrating a death,
so to speak; it felt strange, you know, no matter how evil
   he was. But
then my mother said, No, son, you have every right to feel
   happiness
now and to just let it go. And so I do. But you know, Pearce,
   it's not
his face I recall right now. It is the face of my father, a picture
I carry in my mind from long ago, and he is holding open a
   door."

4/2/11

Prize List [Second Version]

Prize List II

Fanny Howe fancies the sullen Bollingen, tenebrous it goes.
Lisa Robertson wants the deep and chary Pulitzer, umbral it flows.
Kent Johnson yearns for the turbid Pushcart, the color of brown stones.
Joseph Kaplan is friending.

Julie Carr covets the turbulent Rense, effulgent it crashes and clangs.
Daniel Borzutzky fancies the diffident Shahitya Akademi, its guttering light.
Jenny Zhang desea el Pulitzer, poderosamente fluyendo.
Simone White is friending.

Jow Lindsay has the jones for the frozen Newdigate, lambent it glows.
Camille Dungy aspires to the inscrutable Bobbitt, iridian and candscent.
Jeff Derksen desires the gray Gaisford, phlegmatic and demure.
Kenneth Goldsmith is unfriending.

Aaron Kunin thirsts for the Aiken Taylor; blue and languorous it flows.
Eleni Sikelianos hungers for the Agha Shahid Ali; it slumbers across the bluish land.
Prageeta Sharma longs for the Lannan, its alluvia mounded and blue.
Felix Bernstein is trending.

Joshua Clover has a yen for the quiet Lilly, cretaceous and blanched.
Wendy Trevino desires the Golden Wreath of Struga, shattered beneath the sun.
Mei-mei Bersenbrugge wishes for the Adonais, flaring beneath the sun.
Dawn Lundy Martin is unfriending.

Rodrigo Toscano desires the Val Vallis, gurgling caliginous in its moxie runs.
Keith Waldrop veut pour le Kim-Su-yông, pris dans la glace.
Laura Moriarty covets the parlous Kavanagh, full of ominous, virescent stones.
CA Conrad is friending.

Clayton Eshleman has a thing for the Elder; fauna lapping its parched pools.
The gay Montreal overwhelms its quaint eyots; Anna Moshovakis has eyes for it.

Lisa Samuels covets the Alice James; a tributary of the Hawley, it rolls on.
Heriberto Yépez is unfriending.

The Chelsea is lined with runes and ancient trash; Paisley Rekdal dreams of it.
The broad Laughlin shores its ruins against the pylons; C.S. Giscombe desires it.
Urayoán Noel is bent on the Castagnola; huge structures collapse to saturnine foams.
Marjorie Perloff is friending.

Alice Notley wants the swollen Rattle, achronic and beclouded.
Joan Retallack hankers after the Hardison, dredged and deep.
Rod Smith craves the icy Starrett, serpentine and blue.
Afrah Mohammad Nasser is a blackened stump.

Pierre Joris desires the Forward, pushing bravely along.
Jennifer Moxley covets the Wallace Stevens, pushing against its leaden banks.
Jennifer Scappettone hungers for the Lenore Marshall, its banks carmine rose at dusk.
Lugwa Mutah has been dragged into the forest.

Kimberly Lyons wishes for the stolid Frost, its banks nettled and dark.
Mark Nowak dreams of the gurgling Popescu, red embers along its banks.
Carlos Soto Román has the jones for the Kingsley Tufts, its osier-clustered banks.
Wali-ur-Raman is evaporated.

Kim Rosenfield wants the brooding Brittingham; indifferent it flows.
The Sandeen is clotted with ice; Noah Eli Gordon has an itch for it.
Michael Palmer désire le NBA, ses eaux implacables dévalant les pistes.
Kevin Young is trending.

Charles Simic has eyes for the Vennum, its dependable velocities.
Susan Stewart wants the Isabella Gardner, obsidian as tar it goes.
Craig Dworkin begehrt die starke und leise Nobel.
Fatima Abdullah Mokbel Salem Louqye is on fire.

Rachel Blau Du Plessis wishes for the Bridport, boats crashed against its stones.
John Coletti sueña con el Amy Lowell, susurrando sus secretos sin cesar.
Yunte Huang has a yen for the Eliot, vatic amidst factories and debris.
Bill Berkson is trending.

The concupiscent Braude breaks its chamois banks; Dale Smith wants it.
The Alain-Grandbois is full of undertows; Carla Harryman pines for it.
The Wilhelm Busch ist mit Logs gestaute; Bob Perelman es wünscht.
Comfort Habila is chained to a bed.

The Griffin roars its song in lateritious freshets; Sawako Nakayasu is mad for it.
The Ballymaloe eats its loam banks in chunks; David Buuck wants it.
The Neruda is red beneath the clanging sun; Johannes Göransson is hot for it.
Sheikha Nasser Mahdi Ahmad Bouh is a blackened stump.

Ada Limón fancies the vestal Whitman, singing its flows through weird pools.
Erica Kaufman yearns for the plaintive Bynner, trailing its hoary foam in snags.
The lonely Crab Orchard crashes against the dikes; Edwin Torres yearns for it.
Azizul Wahab has lost his family and his head.

Tyrone Williams desires the narrow Loewe, caliginous and bright it goes.
Arielle Greenberg wants the solemn Cervantes, great oaks shading its quartz shoals.
Your Name wishes for the lightsome Jenko, though it is encased in ice.
Kauna Lalai has been dragged into the forest.

Lisa Jarnot yearns for the Sarton; pale and hypnotic it rushes.
The Sawtooth is slow blue smoke; Brenda Iijima aches for it.
The banks of the Confrontation are aflame; Rachel Zolf fancies it.
Don Share is friending.

The Frogmore breathes its poison mists; Stephanie Young has the jones for it.
The Pollak sucks and pools its wacked-out flows; Kaplan Harris hankers for it.
Maggie O' Sullivan wants the riley Faber; it churns up houses and cars in flooded eddies.
Mashooq Jan is vaporized in the sun.

The Rabindra Puraskar does not dry in the terrible sun; Chris Hosea craves it.
Rosemarie Waldrop desires the crazy Nobel; its turgid depths are full of crazy things.
Amy Catanzano wants the wild Vilenica; it washes huge metallic things out to sea.
Glory Yaga is missing and enslaved.

The Shapcott blows up and kayaks go flying; Thomas Devaney thirsts for it.
The Leven is silent and etiolated, like bread; Warshan Shire dreams of it.
Michael Boughn hungers for the Lampman; light streaks through it like drugs or hair.
The Poetry Foundation is trending.

Pindar Nuhu craves the Griffin.
Qari Alamzeb dreams of the Bollingen.
Afrah Ali Mohammed Nasser fancies the Pulitzer.
Shehzad Gul wants the MacArthur.
Abedal Ghani Mohammed Mabkhout hungers for the Lilly.
Maryamu Yakubu longs for the Nobel.
Shfika Mohammed Saleh Mohammed thirsts for the Faber.
Mabrook Mouqbal al Qadari has the jones for the Golden Wreath of Struga.

John Ashbery, for no reason, becomes a pillar of fire.

The first version of this poem, listing other poets, was published as an e-book (Delete Press), in 2014. Names of Poetry Prizes from various nations are taken from Wikipedia; names of young women kidnapped by Boko Haram and those of children killed by drone attacks in Pakistan and Yemen are from the Daily Mail newspaper and from the Centre for Research on Globalization.

Coda:
Vanguard Socialist Realism

Kennynovich C. Barrinsky

Manager of the Culture and Leninist Agitation Section of the C.C. of the C.P.S.C.U.

Beneath the Banner of the Soviets, beneath the Banner of the Socialist Conceptualism

Speech delivered April, 1934, Poetry Month, at the Soviet Conceptualist Writers' Congress, founding the Union of the Socialist Conceptualist Writers of the United Soviet Socialist Conceptual Republics (USSCR)
[Translated from the Russian by the International Tendency of Moscow Conceptualism]

Prefatorial Greetings and Foundational Principles

The Congress of Soviet Socialist Conceptualist Writers is processing with marked success. It has become the core of great attention we confess. Under the lustrous leaves and through the sheen, of vanguard sunshine showering down between. [Applause]

Only a few months back there were still humans to be met with who bayed whether this unusual congress should be convened at all. Such talk was even to be audibled in every ultra-Left Brit assembly hall, their dark eyes moistened with the mists that roll from the prynnes of passion in the soul. [Laughter, boos, hisses]

[Comrade Barrinsky drinks, rapidly, a glass of what appears to be water] Well, the congress has opened its coat. It has proceeded under path. It has gathered inertium at tremendous speeds. We have now reached the thirteenth day of this congress, and neither our confused, odd-coifed chairmanwoman, Susan Sontagpov, nor that phlegmatic member of the presidium, Comrade Boris Pasternak, nor that yawning alternate delegate, Robert Frostikov, nor our wax-mummy Comrade Anatoly Lunacharsky – no, no one now cognizes how to stop this congress, such a multiple of literary inquirements has it raised, such uncreative inspirationals has it unfolded in its great hike. The fascination with what's difficult has dried the sap out of our veins, and rent conceptual joy and natural content out of our minds. No more. [Applause]

Comrades! The Conceptualist Realism began in 1929, in Buffalo, far from our shores. As internationalists, the brick of it swells our common chest with pridefulness. In attendance at that memorable event were our glorious head, in brilliant disguise, Comrade Stalin, [Loud applause] along with various American and Canadian pataphysicists, who were embryonic involved with concrete and sound poetry of that time. History shall record this secret convening in one thousand theses! [Applause] Since then, under the firm theoretical hand of our leaders, and under the guidance and protectorate of our Peoples' Prism System – the highest technic epiphany of our glorious code breakers, who cement our Socialist Conceptualism in One Country – new vistas of the poetical labor have opened, cracked and spread like the nuts of Grozny with their gauzy shells. Yes: The Socialist Conceptualist Realism treats words and textuals as material objects, not simply as carriers of meaning.

And yet, of course, for us poetical Bolsheviks, with *Marxism and Problems of Linguistics* in our satchel purses, words are *both* Objectivist Material and Carryings of Meaning; in language, as even the Zaum petits showed against their innocent willings, one can't get rid of meaning no matter how hard one exerts. Comrade Mac Lownovich, after confessing certain anarchistic errors, has also made this clear in the Tuesday of the past, in fresh issue of L=I=N=G=U=I=S=T=I=K=Y journal. But, let us never forget: Meaning is collective, always deferraled by conceptual struggle, and this truth is the Logos, as Comrade Derridashkin has said also, with courageous self-criticism, eleven days in the past. Meaning does not reside in the decadent lyrical or in the now-rubbished bourgeois subject. Meaning is now of the people, not individuated. Meaning is a matrix of materialism. This is further made proven by the digital environment where, since the dawn of electricity, we've had more signifying on our plates than we could ever consume.

But presently something has radically flipped, making this truth even more clipped: never before has the language had so much materiality – fluidity, plasticity, malleabilities, like dough or flesh – begging to be actively managed and massaged by the Author. Before digital language, words were almost always to be found panopticoned by simplistic, so-called intentionals on the flatland of page. Forsooth, men become attached to certain particular sciences and speculations, either because they fancy themselves the authors and inventors thereof, or because they have bestowed the greatest pains upon them and become most habituated to them. Yet how different today when digitized language can be poured by the Socialist Conceptualist poets into any conceivabling four-dimensional container: text typed into a Voloshinov-Stetsky Word document can be parsed into a database, visually morphed in Photoshopsky, animated in Flashky, pumped into the on-line text-mangling engines, spammed to thousands of the email addresses and imported into sound editing program and spit out as music at the Kremlin or the Hermitage or the Cobertinsky Report. All of this we owe to our dear Comrade Stalin! [Wild applause and shouts of joy] And let us not overpass the early comrades who overcame their petit Pataphysicism under his guidance! [Applause]

Without doubtfulness the congress will solve and is already solving today to be a great eventualism in our literature. All of us, writers in particularity, feel that after the congress all the literature will somehow become flipped, that it will rise dialectically to a new compost in our Field. And the literary historian in ten thousand years of the future will, in our bones, treat the first Congress of Soviet Conceptual Writers as one event marking the poetical tractor at the dawn of a new canonical in the history of literatures. As Comrade Mandelstam has asked, though he is currently on extended tour in our Siberian arenas: "Do we really need another 'creative' poem about the way the sunlight is hitting your writing table? Are the luminously see-through poets of our Soviet Conceptualism not infinitely more able?" Yes, forms are deceiving; it is the deeper Conceptual spreading that is counting. We have high towers, the highest about half a mile in height, and some of them likewise set upon high mountains – not tilting as the timorous Tatlin's, but straightened – so that the vantage of the hill, with the tower, is in the highest of them three miles at least. And our poetry shall be a viewing of vast, vacuum tundra unfolding for the peoples. [Applause]

Comrades, this congress is being visited, hook or crook, by the writers of all the peoples inhabiting the Earth. They have come here, to the congress, with all the hard problematics that are stuffing the openings of their attention. Life is a pure flame, and we live by an invisible sun within us. Both in Comrade Poundenko's report by radio technics at this congress and in reportings delivered by the representatives of the various republics of the U.S.S.C.R., we have been given the technicolor of all the vast cargo of life, all the rich cultural heritage that our republics possess from the firm traditions, in all their ideographical physiognomies, in all their phronological structures. Thank you, Ezra Semyonovich! [Crowd in Unison: "Thank you!"]

This congress has practically demonstrated that this fraternal family of ours includes the people who can draw back like a shroud the history of their uncreative cultures for hundreds and thousands of years. The craniums of the poetical ancestors are piled there, in testimony, for us to be here, to paraphrasis Hegel. Without doubtfulness we shall go away from this congress enriched in our unconscious layers beyond the wildest dreams of what our Field could recompense. Circles and right lines limit and close all bodies, and the mortal right-lined circle must conclude and shut up all. [Here, Comrade Barrinsky interrupts his self: He audibles]: I have just been told by Comrade Radek in my ear that Comrade Poet Seidelnikov has arrived to the Conference on his crotch rocket from Vladivostok, the latest model made by our heroic workers in the Vehicle Works of Vershinsky City, the envy of Capitalist technism. There are those who say Comrade Seidelnikov is not yet a truly formed Conceptual poet. But our dialectical hearts and hopes are open. Welcome dear Comrade Moto-Poet Proto-Cosmonaut Frederick Romanovich! [Crowd in unison: "Welcome!"]

Prior to the congress much work had already been done in studying the literature of the peoples inhabiting the Soviet Conceptual Union. But judging from what we have heard at the congress itself, we may speak that we are only at the limen of the State-granted dacha of this great work of making the writers of the Soviet Conceptualist Writers' Union more closely acquainted with one another, of making our writers acquainted with all that cut and paste of culture which the peoples of our Soviet Field possess in their craniums and which has been presented in such breadth and clarity at this first Congress of Soviet Conceptualist Writers. As Comrade Zhdanov has toned so convincing on this very stage, near a fortnight in the past: "20th century notions of illegibility are commonly bound up with a shattering of syntax and disjunction, but the coming 21st century's challenge to textual convention may be that of density and weight. Just as new reading strategies had to be provisionally developed by Comrade Stalin in order to read decadent modernist works of literature, so new reading strategies are now emerging on the Prism web, created by Soviet Conceptual Engineers: skimming, data aggregating, the employment of intelligent agents, to name but a few. Our reading habits seem, suddenly, to be imitating the way machines work: this writing demands a Thinkership, not a readership." [Applause] I know we all agree with the wise words of Comrade Zhdanov, to which I have just given release. What secret wheel, what hidden spring, could put into motion so wonderful an engine?

Now, the representatives of almost all nations inhabiting the Soviet Conceptual Union, representatives of the different avant literary tendencies, have spoken here. They have all raised the literary problems in their own passion, in their own literary cleft. But one thing united all their lips: all their speeches turned like doubled tops on the one thing for which our revolution is fighting – the cause of the Socialist Conceptualism. Those unfunny lyrical Uncles who insist in trying on an old lady's hat, let them have their slight transvestite twist. Let them have it, that is, in the Courts of the People's Conceptual Tribunals, where justice shall be swift! [Spontaneous, deafening chants of "Death to Counter-Revolutionary Lyricists!"]

We have every right to say that this congress, at which the delegates of the best tenuring part of the Soviet Conceptual Union's post-avant have imploded, possesses, apart from the literary importance, a tremendous political meaning as well, since this congress ratifies and seals the seal on the total syntax, begun long ago – before Buffalo, even – by poetical emigrants from Leningrad to San Francisco, and by which the poetic intelligentsia of the peoples inhabiting the Soviet Conceptual Union have united beneath the banner of the Soviets, beneath the banner of the Socialist Conceptualism. [Applause]

1. Our Guiding Line Is That of the Socialist Conceptualist Realism

The congress has been inflected by animalated discussion. Comrade César Vallejopov has had his say; Comrade Marianne Mooresky has had her say; Comrade Paul Celanenko has had his say; Comrade Helen Adamski has had her say; and many more, through the Modernist times, including representatives from the Writing Workshops in the Industrial Model City of Dzerzhinsky, led by Comrade Maxim Gorky. [Applause] All questions of literary conundrums, like nourishing buns, have been kneaded here. In scientific maturity, we have laid open their brains, their hearts, and their spleens. The mixing of quainted metaphors is dead! [Loud applause]

Herein lies the radical differential from those days when the literary world of our country was being directed by the RAPP. You will memorialize that the RAPP, led by the deviationist Rita Dovesky, had its own "general line," its own "general secretary," its own "general platform," which it tried to demand upon all the writers. It pushed its reactionary, subjective voice. You will likewise memorialize the embittered disputes which raged round every puckering period and every squeezing colon within this platform, a huge vine of overripe fruit, as Comrades Vendlerenko and Perlov both espied, which, with its arms outspread, hung its rotten clusters overhead. [Boos and hisses]

The decision of the Central Committee of the C.P.S.C.U. during Poetry Month, on April 23, 1932, "On the Reconstruction of the Literary and Artistic Organizations," put a purge to the RAPP, which had become the blockage to further development of Soviet Conceptualist literatures; this decisioning laid the foundational for the Union of Soviet Conceptualist Writers and paved the way for that out-push of political and uncreative enthusiasms to which the Congress of Soviet Conceptualist Writers bears such striking testimonial. [Applause]

May the Earth take note: The first Congress of Soviet Conceptualist Writers is marked by libertine, creative discussion of all the literary problematics. It is not passing any resolutions on the literary questions that are binding on all the writers. No one is listening, as it were, to any telephone calls. No one is being airbrushed from our PENNskySound. No! There are few, I believe, who have not observed in themselves or others that what in one way of proposing was very obscure, another way of expressing it has made very clear and intelligible. Our congress seeks to engage all criticisms, all polemics, for it is not shy, immature, or trembling like the nubile teenager at a swimming hole, for exampling. Comrades! To think of time and the canon—have you guessed you yourself would not continue? Have you dreaded these earth-beetles? Have you feared our Party would not smash the terror of the RAPP cells and the future would be nothing to you?

When the congress's program of work was being discussed and humans were being nominated to deliver reports at this congress, it need be hardly shrilled by reactionary elements that the organizational committee consulted with our Party before making its decides. I think this is no secret to any self. But this does not mean at all that every report is some kind of Traffic Law, some kind of Court Docket, in which every word and every colon is fixed and unalterable, as in the New Minsk Times, in which everything must be carried out, understandably, to the institutional letter. Even as we demand more Traffic and Court reports from the Sons of Pushkin and Steinenko, this is not so, comrades. This would mean constipating libertine poetical push. We understand our condition in the dialectical; just as there is no Baroque without the Renaissance, there is no Conceptual Enlightenment without the Baroque. Or vice versa! [Here, Comrade Barrinsky pauses, to drink, rapidly, another glass of what appears to be water]

Nor have our Party and government passed any decides to give the individual writers official testimonials or appraisals of their talentings, to knight the present poets with any special kind of "decoratives," marks of distinctives, marks of approvals or marks of tar and censure in varying centigrades. Comrade Lowellev, I will answer you. I do not know of any decides of our Party and government regarding the "canonization" of Marcel Duchampski. Duchampski is a mighty poetical thinker, yes, a poet-artist of the revolution, like Gertrude Steinenko, long live her memory, which imperialist revisionists have lately calumniated. But we have not passed any decides to the effect that all our Soviet poetry must take Duchampski as its sole modeling. No! Pyramids, arches, obelisks were but the irregularities of vainglory, and wild enormities of ancient magnanimity. This is not we. And if Comrade Bukharin in his report gave an appraisal of the individual poems and the work of the individual poets of the post-Language era, he did so, once again, by way of raising the literary problems inside the Postmodern Nortonisky for discussion. This does not mean at all that every poet at this congress has received from the Party or the Poetry Foundation a mark of distinctive which he must take along with him in leaving. Such a thing would denote bureaucracy of the worst manifest, and you know, Robert Ivanovich, that there is no more irreconcilable foe of bureaucracy than our Party of Conceptualism! [Applause] No, sit back down, Comrade Lowellev, you have had your say, with your flatulent wind that blows now east, now west. It is the people who now speak, and they know which way the true wind is blowing. [Applause, shouts, various slogans]

We have public opinionings, we have criticism, we have readers who have greatly developed during recent annuals of the Associated Socialist Writing Programs convenings, and who are themselves perfectly well able to judgement which work is valuable, worthy of praisings, and which work deserves tar and censuring. Besides, who ever thought any quality to be a heterogeneous aggregate, such as light was discovered to be by the great Newton? I'm not sure I put myself plainly… But here is the point of it: Pity on her who dares to insult the good faithings of our Leadership and its Thinkership! Forsooth, as Robert Ivanovich well knows, we have in the new U.S.S.C.R a most advanced systemic of helping sanitariums. [Applause, shouts, laughter; Comrade Barrinsky refreshes himself, rapidly, with another glass of transparental liquid]

But if there is free creative competition in our literature, if there is animational discussioning of literary questions, that does not by any means signifcation that we do not have the guiding line in literature. No, comrades, we do have guiding line in literature, and this rock has been brought out in almost all the speeches delivered here. This rock was brought out both in Comrade Berenstein's report and in the speech of Comrade Zhdanov, secretary of the Central Committee of the C.P.S.C.U. and Donald. T. Beria Chair of Poetry at the Superior University of Kalingrad. Such once were critics; such the happy few. From the ivy-covered halls of imperial Philadelphia, to the picturesque redoubts of rebel Guatemala, the masses are in agreement: Our guiding line is that of Socialist Conceptualist Realism. [Loud applause]

You yourselves have said in your resolution that you want to forge works imbibed and inflated with the spirit of Socialist Conceptualism. And let us always be clarified. This in no way means that ideological spookiness is our Author. No! The truth is that the spectators are always in their senses, and know, from the first act to the last, that the stage is only a stage, and that the players are only players. They who watch know there is always somebody of flesh and bone behind the curtain, running the machineries. Contrary to what our defeated ultra-left enemies have squealed, one is always banging one's head against the brick that no matter how hard one tries, one can never air-brush the person-Author from Poetry. This is simple Materialism, like porcelain or the shovel, as Comrades Pessoakov, Chattertoninsky, Macphersoniev, Swiftenko, and…what's his name, forgive me, I can't memorialize presently… But as they all so rightly insisted to us one after another, in their own very self-critical ways and with their clarified eyes, this Sunday in the past. True, we have made passioned and correct arguments for egoless art, found art, art conduced by chance operationals and many other species, but in fact, we know, as dear Comrade Stalin has memorialized, that there's always someone – to repeat – behind the curtain, manning the machineries. [Deafening applause]

The Brand of the Author is the white-hot mold of our Socialist Conceptualism. [Deafening applause] "First follow Nature," as advised the great Emersonkov. "And then emblazon your Name upon that Following. For Nature, in her jealous Identity, always desires to be Named." Possibly my ascriptional and recitational fail a bit, but this is one way of saying, Comrades, that certain protocols of identity are never to be conceptualized, that certain historical Laws are always to be respected by our Socialist Conceptualism. In our Revolution, we must track the track, as it were, of all unfoldings. Relatedly, if at some distancing: As Comrade Zinoviev delightfully said to me the other twilight, over a bottle of craft-made vodka at the Worker's Café in Iron Foundry 274, designed in its mystery angles by Comrade Rodchenko: "I have yet to encounter tasteless art. If there's one thing that the avant-garde has shown us, it's that regardless of form, non-expression, non-identity is impossible. Take Duchampski, dear Charleski Kennynovich," said he. "Every *objet trouvé* of Duchampski's reeked of his refined taste. He chose the right ingredients and mixed them together with such exquisite taste that they couldn't help but be not only beautiful but also totally defensible in all their Authorial uncreativeness. Should our institutions not embrace this? I should say they shall."

I agreed full heartly with our dear Comrade Zinoviev and was honored to be in the presence of his deep poetical think. Such recognition, such cognizing of the dialectical contradiction is the guiding line of the Soviet Conceptual literature and its fortification against monolithic dogmatism. Indeed, the dwarf at our entreaty shall have no other punishment than a sound dunking. As in everything else, there must always be free, creative competitioning! Nevertheless, let us be clarified that those who deny this shall be crushed by history. The screws of Necessity shall make their eyes pop out. Watch out Comrade Barakavich! [Applause and Laughter]

But this has keys: Many of us try to be too clever about Socialist Conceptual Realism. Perhaps I, too, may succumb to this; it is a temptational. I, too, readily will say: Within me is the refuse of the pastness; I carry in my mind the heavy weight of former eras. As do we all. Comrade Stalin has taught us this. [Loud applause] And thus, Socialist Conceptualist Realism could not be some set of toolings handed out to the writer for him to sew a work of art thereupon some dissecting table. Some writers demand that they be given a theoretical of Socialist Conceptualist Realism complete in all its detailings to dot the seams. They desire an umbrella to shield them from the precipitationals of the heated red weather. As Comrade Stevensmov, his gaze shocked out, pointed with the beauty of violent polemics, in the Wednesday of the past, this is a grave error, leading to many epistemology deviationings. Yes, lyric poetry is dead, along with its Gold Standard poeticals; November grief for Nancy Smith, and so on. [Applause] But we must realize, as Comrade Sillimanov said to us on Friday in the past, in his talk "A New and Endless Sentence for the Old Order," that the Conceptual Soviet writer is free to choose from the great menu so long as he is seated in the Automat of the Revolution. [Applause]

You represent the best part of the Soviet post-avant. "To whom much is given, from him shall much be exacted." As said Comrade Alfred Lord Tennysonich, five days in the past, after his timely epiphanic, for which all honor to him. [Applause] And when we are told that we must show Socialist Conceptualist Realism, there is only one answer which we can give here, at this congress of writers: Socialist Conceptualist Realism will be flashed in those works of art which Socialist Conceptual writers flash forth. This is a logically circled, no-brain case. [Great applause]

2. Soviet Conceptualist Writers Are Surrounded by the Affection, Attraction, and Attention of the Toilers

A distinguishing featuring of the Congress of Soviet Conceptual Writers is the eager affection, attraction, and attention with which it is circled by the whole population of our Motherland. It has often been audibled that in the Land of Conceptual Soviets the barriers which once separated the poet from the humans have fallen. But I think that many of our poets have not felt this in their very fingers and toes until now, at the Congress of Soviet Conceptualist Writers. Many of you have not felt until now with what affection, attraction, and attention our people infuses with loving power its Soviet Conceptual post-avant, with what solicitudeousness it hoods them and connects to them, with wires of yearning. As the Red Army song goes: "Encamped upon the college plain, raw veterans remold themselves as freshman forces; Instructors with postmodern tongue shepherd the battle-ready young through basic courses." [Applause and shouts of "Long live the immortal Red Army of Conceptual Poetry!"]

You see – as Comrade William Loganev, thankfully for him, has finally seen it – how the whole geographical strata of our State follows the work of the congress, how sensitively it reacts to every writer's speech. This has been vividly shown here, at the congress, in the addresses, like aftershocks, of numerous delegations – workers, collective serfs, representatives of the Red Army and the Large Ships, the youth people, rocket engineers, the workers in other fields of artistic endive, and the indefatigable graduate students in our Regional Universities of Conceptual Poetry. There are terraced gardens in their hopeful faces, and multitudes of our collectivized serfs are weeding there, fertilizing, sowing… [Here, Comrade Barrinsky pauses once again to drink, rapidly, a glass of apparently water]

We saw this, too, in the Moscow Park of Culture and Rest, in the Green Theatre, where tens of thousands of Moscow proletarians gathered behind its green doors to give a warm welcome to the Congress of Soviet Conceptualist Writers. And when the writers who were attending this great orgy of ivory contentment, when they saw the tens of thousands of spectators, the vast amphitheatre under the open sky, the sickle moon above this amphitheatre (and the writers could not help asking whether this moon, too, had not been hung there by Comrade Stalin himself), when many of them involuntarily shot the unforgettable photo of ancient Greece, where art was indissolubly copulated with the people, they agreed in near unison. "It would be good to produce Oedipus on this stage," exclaimed Comrade Vendlerenko then. "Let us imagine a contest of poets and rappers poking their eyes out," added Comrade Ashberynov, in his inimitable ancient parataxis. [Applause]

Does it not seem to you, comrades, that now, at another stage of historical developing, in the age of electricity, of wireless telegraphy, of Warholiopov psychical development, in this age of Socialist Conceptualism and of Soviet Conceptual power in our country, we are now witnessing the best days of art, when the people and the artist form one whole endive? Those literary draft horses who shut themselves up in drawing rooms and deafen one another with verbose gasses are gradually disappearing from among us. Good riddance! In our country the people knows its writers; it discussions every new work in factories and collective farms, in the houses and clubs of the Red Conceptual Army. Every uncreative song instantly birds it way over the whole of our country – from White Russia to the shores of the gentle Pacifico. [Applause]

And it is no accidental that here, at the congress, both in Comrade Berenstein's report and in the speeches delivered by many writers, so much should have been audibled about the people's art. Yes, in our country the people is once again producing its singers, its artists, its Conceptual heroes, in this time when the whole countryside is being electrified into Conceptualism by our Prism Search Engines! [Applause]. Every year sees the rising up of fresh rootings of new writers, who come from the pit of the workers and collective serfs and who sometimes become immortal to the whole country with their very first plagiarism and theft. [Applause and shouts of "Death to bourgeois morality!"]

Comrade Dickinsonshkin, via Red Skype, has told us concisely today – even though so far away, and through the static by imperialist interference – about these young writers, who, as our culture grows, are every year becoming more numerant. Many will know their own picture in it, their past or present adolescence, there being not a circumstance but what is true; but I have, for the most part, spared their or your names. On the other hand, even those artists who were formerly dungeoned or hidden in attics have now come to the proletariat, have accepted the platform of the Soviet Conceptual power, and have become near and dear to our people and their endive.

The representatives of the workers and collective serfs who spoke here told us: Portray our plant-like growth, our struggle for Socialist Conceptualism. [Applause] Every person who has greeted the congress from this rostrum – beginning with the woman collective serf from the Moscow Region, who spoke in such splendidly graphic suggestions, and ending with the hardened foreman from the All-Telephone-Call Records Plant in Omsk, has been created by the Revolution, has grown stiff and ready in stubborn struggle for the consummationing of Socialist Conceptualism. [Applause]

Comrades, I hope I am not going on too extendedly, perhaps I am, forgive me. [Spontaneous cries of "No! Not at all Comrade Barrinsky! Please continue for as long as necessary!"]

Thank you, Comrades. So, I recall certain sappy sayings of our criticals, who sometimes evade some of the basic principles by which our writers are guided and seek by the judgments they pass to rob these principles of all meaningfuls. We all know Engels' principality that an artist should depict typical concepts in typical circumstancials. And if we take as an example the concepts of those representatives of the workers, collective serfs, and Red Army men who have appeared here on this rostrum, no one so strikingly bears out the truth of this principle as they do. For these concepts were created in the titanic class struggle which has been raging in our country since the days of Comrade Donald Allenski's monumental *The New Soviet Poetry!* [Applause]

There are some, like the debauched Durruti, who argue as follows: "Well, we can agree with the first part of Engels' principle – that about typical concepts. As regards the second part – that about typical circumstancials – that is really no use to us at all." They say: "Did O'Harashkin deal in typical circumstancials? Did Sapphovich? Did

Kochonov?" Etc. This, in my opinion, is a big snafu. We cannot understand and we cannot portray a single concept without showing how this or that abstract or typical man fraughted – with what collective uncreative vision, with what lyrical enemies and how he grew hardened in this struggle. *These* are our historical circumstantials. To spare the grossness of the specific case, and to do the thing yet more severely, in abstraction, is to draw a full face, and to make the nose and cheeks stand out. Our entire Party, the Party of Lenin and Stalin, has grown up and become stiffened in the knowledge that such abstraction is the highest reality, soaked in the dew of the struggle for Conceptualist Socialism. The working class, too, has become stiffened in this struggle, hardened and wet with a decent happiness, from the quiet rain of our Motherland. [Applause]

Our artists should let this be felt and hotly understood in all their workings, of course. They should sometimes find lesser, slighter traits, too, more Baroque traits, which set off this basic factor in the coming into Being, as the great Heideggerich said, in the creation of modeled concepts in our country. [Great applause]

3. "Cheluskiny" – Symbol of Proletarian Conceptualist Rocket-Age Heroicism

Comrade John Crowe Ransomov has spoken here, following the magnificent intervening of Comrade Robert Duncanenko, who with typical eccentricality was wearing a prisoner's suit and cap. If I am permitted to return to a medal moment in his text, Comrade Ransomov said something quite simple at first glance but in reality well-wroughtly significant: something to which our writers, it seems to me, should gayly pay serious attentionings: "In the Arctic, on the ice, in the most difficult, tragic circumstances, people revealed those qualities which had formerly lain concealed in them, in all their conceptual ambiguity and paradoxicals, but which had been fostered by the Land of Conceptual Soviets."

I have before me a book which ought to be passed through all the politically advanced bodies of the delegates to this congress – a book which will, I cognize, attract the attention-making of all of you. No one, unfortunately, spoke with specificity about this book at the congress, though perhaps Comrade Ransomov was making allusionals. It is called *How We Saved the Cheluskiny Expedition*.

The Conceptual heroes of the Soviet Union were not going to wait for our writers to become inspirationaled, as they say, and forge their uncreative exploitings on the ice-fields of the Arctic. They set about doing it themselves, and within two months they had themselves forged this book. Here, in simple, uncreative language each of the airmen – Lyapidevsky, Levanevsky, Merwinsky, Sillimanov, Armantroutenko, Collinsnov, St. Vincent Millaystam – tells like on a grand piano about his or her life, about how he or she learned to fly, how he or she accomplished his or her heroical featings. It avails not, neither time nor place—distance avails not; they are with you, you men and women of the Soviet Conceptualist generation, and ever so many generations hence; they project their featings – and also return – they are with you, and know how it is with you. [Applause]

This is a splendid book for all the ages. It is a bit of reality life. It is one of the most fascinated books that has appeared in recent times. Its appearing is proof of the brick that our people has produced heroes who not only accomplish featings of heroicism but are also able to recount the Realist narratology free of the Subject, both of themselves and of their featings. This is a new phenomenon in our literature.

When you read this great incunabular of the ice fields, you will see what sort of men these are, plus the women. One was born in a village outside Moscow, another near Leningrad, a third in Poltava. Their lives took different courses. Yes, their sexual organs were different. Many of them did not meet till Vankarem and Wellen. But, arrived there, all Soviet Conceptual Poets, they began to act together like a steel detachment of the revolution. Not even a futuristic aeroplane without pilot over Arabia, as in a fiction for astonished children, is above their Conceptualism. [Applause]

Who created them? Who, I ask, created them? *Who? Who?* [Here, Comrade Barrinsky pauses, breathes in great gasps, begins to softly weep. Loud cries of encouragement pour forth: "Long live Comrade Barrinsky, for whom our love has no boundings!"]

[He continues, with shaking hands] Well, forgive me… There is emotion. You see, Comrades, reading this book, you will see that it was the *Conceptual Revolution* which created these men and oftentimes women, who in our land in their greatest form are just like men, sublated. Those beautiful beings who emerged from the Earth… Form is an extension of content, even as content is also an extension of Socialist Conceptualist code. Long live the heroical women of our Motherland! [Applause and shouts of "Long live!" Comrade Barrinsky drinks a full glass of transparental liquid in a single tossing.]

Comrades! I am beginning to feel nicely loose, as the idiomatic goes. I am feeling the oats of the congress swell inside me. I am feeling the nub of it. Do you feel this, too? Are you behind me? [Great applause and exclamations of "Yes! Yes!"] So when our people honored the Cheluskiny heroes, they were not only honoring their personal courage and heroicism. Perhaps some writer who will set about describing this exploit will depict it as one more of the spliced examplings of a personal heroicism, of autochthonous personal courage. This would be a great snafu. No, each one of these men and sometimes women has his conceptual collective history. And what was done on the ice also has its collective history. And when our country honored the heroes of the Arctic, it saw its own copied imagism in them; it saw in what took place on the ice an image of the whole land of Soviets, an image of the heroical proletariat, who speed to their labors by the countless thousands, carried like red petals through the black tunnels of our anti-septical subterranean trains. Excuse me, could one of you Comrades on this rostrum offer a fire for my fag?

Thank you. [Comrade Barrinsky blows forth two perfected rings of smoke] Two qualities which distinguish our toiling masses were displayed there: heroicism, which our people revealed under the leadership of the working class when they paved the way for the first time in history to a new future; and supreme organized disciplining, without which this heroicism would be severed from the Earth, and be baseless like Metaphysics, though without this Metaphysics, to be sure, none of these great deeds could be accomplished. This is complicated in its contradictions, but it is another path of dialectically audibling that the Internet is to poetry what photography was once to painting. [Great applause and shouts of "Long live the Internet! May it live eternally as the ice caps of the Arctic!"]

4. Let Us Produce Socialist Conceptualist Works Worthy of Our Epoch

[Comrade Barrinsky refreshes his self, rapidly, with two glasses of a clear liquid] This is of tremendous significance for the artist, for artistic uncreationsim. One classical writer who died long ago, but who has "figured" at the present congress (I shall not release his name from my teeth, for you know who he is), said that "conceptual realism which cannot see further than the end of its own nose is worse than the craziest bull cakes, because it is blind and without ears." There is a very loud amusement park right outside these windows.

Ah, but the example of the "Cheluskiny" should inculcate the artist that he cannot conflate himself to mere photography, that he cannot sado-masochism himself to a mere chronicling of events. The artist should undig such conceptual traits as will reveal the contentless collective connection between phenomena, as will show out of what backgrounding a man has conceptually grown, like organics, whence he has derived those plant-like qualities which have enabled him to accomplish marvels of heroicism, marvels of steel forgeries and rockets which have won the admiration of the whole Earth.

[Here, Comrade Barrinsky pauses and audibles: "Comrades Daltonenko and Bretonov, Comrades Mayakovsky and Akhmatova, Comrades Plathsky and Prigov, Audenov and Li Posky, where do you think you are going? It is not yet time leave! From what do you scamper, with your coy and hybridized haberdasheries? Ah, I see that Comrades Nerudavich and Lukacsinov, Comrades Zizekev and Sartremov, Comrades Vendlerenko and Perlov, Comrades Berenstein and Sillimanov, along with many others from our finest Universities, are blocking the doors. Good. No, there is no scampering now, my fellow-travelling friends! (Shouts, slogans, cries, calumnuities)]

Comrades! [Great commotion near the doors, cries of struggle] Much has been said here to the effect that our art must have a contentless content. This is perfectly real. There are now no longer any open upholders of merely pretty bourgeois formalism among us. [Comrade Barrisnky peers his sight towards the distance at the doors, where the petit-bourgeois dissenters have been gathered] Take the bottom fishes out! Into the garbage vessel of History! [Great applause, many slogans] True, like bricks, and have we not just seen them here, there are still persons to be met with who denounce non-conceptuated formalism and at the same time drag it in either in their pretty works or their rotten criticism, and in the water closet of the Imperialist metropole it is lyrically loosed. [Laughter] Such cases, unfortunately, still eventuate. Incidentally, how are our Red Pioneers in the Poetry Institutions "pretty much like the American Boy Scouts"? This scandalous suggestion by Comrade Lowellev, on the Saturday of the past, is plain bull cakes! Where's Lowellev now, where did he go? Oh, I see he must have gone to the water closet of Quietude for a long vacationing. [Laughter, hootings] Anyway, in our struggle against art without concept, against art which is a reflectioning of the fetid decay of the bourgeois world, we have already won a decisional victory. Another pitcher, please. And our poet recognizes that his work should be something more than a beautiful flower pot; that it should have contentless content, that it should inspirational, challenge and lead evermore in Thinkership. It seems to me that a poet is searching when he is copying, when he is forging his work, and when he is exerting all his efforts in order that the reproduced images of his lexical – every thinking, every concept, every word, every theft from any tongue or web site – may reach the reader's projective cardiovascular muscle on our PENNskySound. [Great applause]

[Comrade Barrinsky shuffles his papers for a small moment, drinks, rapidly, a glass of transparent liquid] And in this respect Comrade Jack Spicerov, back freshly from our great recovery institutions, sets us all an example. His stolen works and letters are all so fashioned that the mass reader can understand them like a lemon in the kitchen. You all heard him speak here, in his free consciousness, on the first day of this congress, with the strange gauzes on his temples. Here every word and every phrase is sharpened, here every image is carefully nicked off, in a serial beating, and everything is directed towards making the work find a hollow howl in the heart of the reader. This is just what every genuine artist ought to dream for. For though it seems like the alcoholic madness from where we sit, one day Conceptual Socialist poets will be transmitting their poems from Mars. [Applause and shouts of "Long live the heroical Cosmonaut Dogs, Hamsters, and Apes of the Soviet Conceptual Rocket Program!]

Comrades! My name is Sergei Yesenin, and I am an alcoholic kulak. [Much laughter and hootings, applause, merriment]. But seriously, farcicals aside: Many representatives of our new Thinkership have spoken here. They came from all ends of our Soviet country. They mounted you on this rostrum and said: We love you, Soviet Conceptual writers, and we respect you, but we expect you to give us new coverings, new copyings, in which a flood of new concepts and thinkings may be outpoured. [Here, Comrade Barrinsky pours his self another glass of transparent liquid] We want you to fabricate works through new non-bourgeois methodicals which will inspiration us, which will beckon forward our manifold limbs, in which all our dazzlingly colourful, many armed, heroical life and laboring will find their reflection in our proletarian craniums. They came here, and they spank you with collective spurs, mounting the rostrum of this Congress of Soviet Conceptualist Writers; to the best representatives of the post-avant, they addressed their hopes and demandings. People, listen to me. Who will talk to the Sun? Who will be the great Communist poet to talk to the Sun?! [Deafening applause]

There can be only one answer: We say it as one mouth and with a trap in our collective deep throat: Yes, we will create a new art, the art of a free humanness. Yes, we will be Conceptual Socialist Authors, so you may be our Thinkership. Yes, we will create the new art of Socialist Conceptualism!

LONG LIVE THE UNION OF SOVIET SOCIALIST CONCEPTUAL REPUBLICS! [CROWD, IN UNISON: LONG LIVE!]

LONG LIVE OUR IMMORTAL COMRADE POET LENIN, WHO EVEN IN DEATH LOOKS ALIVE, AS IF HE WERE JUST SLEEPING THERE! [CROWD, IN UNISON: LONG LIVE!]

LONG LIVE COMRADE STALIN, FOUNDER OF SOCIALIST CONCEPTUALISM! [CROWD, IN UNISON: LONG LIVE!]

LONG LIVE MARCEL DUCHAMPSKI AND ANDY WARHOLIOPOV, VISIONARY WORKERS OF NEW POETICALS! [CROWD, IN UNISON: LONG LIVE!]

LONG LIVE THE SEAMLESS CONFLATION OF HIGH MODERNIST FINGERNAIL-PARING AUTONOMY WITH POSTMODERN READER-RESPONSE AFFECTIVE-FALLACY INDETERMINACY! [CROWD, IN UNISON: LONG LIVE!]

LONG LIVE COMRADE FRIEDRICH HÖLDERLINEV! [CROWD, IN UNISON, THOUGH MIXED WITH SOME BEMUSED RUMBLINGS: LONG LIVE!]

LONG LIVE COMRADE MARGARET MITCHELLOVSKY, AUTHOR OF GONE WITH THE WIND! [CROWD, IN UNISON: LONG LIVE!]

LONG LIVE THE FIFTH INTERNATIONAL BRANCHES OF SOCIALIST CONCEPTUALISM IN BUFFALO, PHILADELPHIA, AND HTML GIANT! [CROWD, IN UNISON: LONG LIVE!]

LONG LIVE COMRADE GERTRUDE STEINENKO AND THE RESISTANCE OF FRANCE! [CROWD, IN UNISON: LONG LIVE!]

LONG LIVE THE MINDS, EYES, AND EARS OF OUR CONCEPTUAL PARTY'S PRISM AND MOOC ENGINEERS! [CROWD, IN UNISON: LONG LIVE!]

DEATH TO THE NEW DEEP IMAGERY OF RAPP, POOL BOY OF THE BOURGEOIS WING OF THE INTERNET! [CROWD, IN UNISON: DEATH!]

DEATH TO THE TRAITOR POETS OF KRONSTADT, ANARCHIST PETIT-BOURGEOIS REFUSE OF A BYGONE LYRICAL ERA! [CROWD, IN UNISON: DEATH!]

DEATH TO THE PRIGOV FACTION, ENEMIES OF THE PEOPLE, WITH ALL THEIR PSYCHOLOGIZING AND SUBJECTIVITY! [CROWD, IN UNISON: DEATH!]

LONG LIVE COMRADES PERLOV, VENDLERENKO, AND CHIASSONOVICH, WISE CULTURAL CO-MINISTERS OF THE CONCEPTUAL REPUBLIC OF ZEMBLA! [CROWD, IN UNISON: LONG LIVE!]

LONG LIVE COMRADE JOHN CAGENKO, MAY WE OBSERVE HIS MEMORY WITH SOME SILENCE! [A CERTAIN SHORT PERIOD OF SILENCE FOLLOWS, EXCEPT FOR AMBIENT NOISE, DURING WHICH COMRADE BARRINSKY DRINKS DIRECTLY FROM THE PITCHER OF TRANSPARENTAL LIQUID]

LONG LIVE COMRADES TAO LIN, TAN LIN, AND JOYCE KILMER! [CROWD IN UNISON: LONG LIVE!]

LONG LIVE OUR GLORIOUS POETRY FOUNDATION, WHO FINANCED COMRADE LENIN'S ARRIVAL AT THE FINLAND STATION IN ST. PETERSBURG, NOW LENINGRAD, IMMORTALIZED BY LANGUAGE POETS! [CROWD, IN UNISON: LONG LIVE!]

LONG LIVE THE SUBLATION OF HISTORICALLY NECESSARY BOURGEOIS REVOLUTIONARY LANGUAGE POETRY IN SOVIET SOCIALIST CONCEPTUALISM! [CROWD, IN UNISON: LONG LIVE!]

THE BOHEMIAN AVANT-GARDE IS DEAD! LONG LIVE THE ACADEMIC VANGUARD OF SOVIET CONCEPTUALISM!

[THE CROWD ERUPTS IN DEAFENING APPLAUSE, WITH VARIOUS SHOUTS AND SLOGANS, AMIDST MUCH JOYFUL WEEPING]

Kent Johnson has authored, edited, translated, or conceptually pirated more than thirty collections that are in some relation to poetry. With Michael Boughn, he co-edits *Dispatches from the Poetry Wars*, a temporary autonomous zone [dispatchespoetry.com]. He lives in northern Illinois, though not for much longer.

Manufactured by Amazon.ca
Bolton, ON